The psychology of Attraction Explained

Contents

About the Author

M. Farouk Radwan is the founder of one of the most popular self-help websites on the Internet in terms of traffic. www.2knowmyself.com, the site Farouk founded, has been getting more than one million visits each month at the time this book was published.

Farouk has been studying psychology since he was 17 years old. He has completed several psychology-related degrees, has written thousands of articles and authored 10 books.

Farouk doesn't believe in intuitive tricks or perceptive advice, but he rather focuses on methods that have been proven to be 100% practical through scientific research and which are backed up by scientific fact.

Basic Concepts of Attraction

What's Hardwired and Learned

Can the media affect the way we perceive attractiveness?

Are there universally defined attractive facial features?

Does the perception of attractiveness vary across different cultures?

What makes a person physically attractive? And what makes another person ugly?

Thanks to advances in neuro–science and brain imaging studies, and to the extensive research done by psychologists, it is possible to answer these questions accurately.

Researchers have found that human beings are born with certain pre-coded instructions in their brains. These instructions determine what they find attractive and what they find unattractive. These settings are like the factory default settings a mobile phone or a car comes with.

A car is designed, for example, to display the image of a fuel tank when the fuel is about to run out. In other words, the car was initially programmed to work that way the day it was made.

Just like these cars, human beings are also programmed with certain software that helps them determine who is attractive and who isn't. The main purpose for that software from a design point of view is to help a man and a woman bring the healthiest and the greatest number of offspring into the world.

In addition to these factory default settings human beings come with, they also have a certain capacity for learning and for adding new data. Unlike a car, which cannot be programmed by learning, a human being can actually alter its program right after learning something new.

That's why the way people are raised and the experiences they go through determine, to a certain extent, the people they are going to be attracted to. Or in other words, the new data a human being gets exposed to can alter the way his initial programming works.

For example, men are usually attracted to women who have feminine facial features (according to the hardwired instructions in their brains). However, as a result of the experiences they go through, some men deviate from this norm and are attracted to other features that have nothing to do with their initial programming.

Here is another example:

Women are hard wired to look for resourceful men and to favour the resourceful man over the more attractive one when it comes to long-term relationships (provided that all the other factors are constant). However, women who develop self-image problems (who dislike their looks), sometimes override their factory default just because they want to prove to others they can attract a good looking man. In other words, the woman who wants to date a very attractive man at all costs just to prove that she can, might reject the resourceful man whom she is biologically designed to be attracted to when she seeks a long-term relationship. This doesn't mean that women who always seek good looks have self-esteem issues but it's just an example to show how different variables can determine the type of person we get attracted to.

The perceived attractiveness of some physical features such as body weight, as you will see in the following pages, is determined by the culture people live in. It has been found that a preference for slim women is a cultural preference and not a hardwired instruction in men's brains. This means that people begin to prefer slim women because of new beliefs implemented in their minds by the media and their society.

So, in short, what attracts one person to another is a combination of the hardwired information the person was born with, along with any programming that he has received along the way, which adds, removes, or modifies anything in the initial programming.

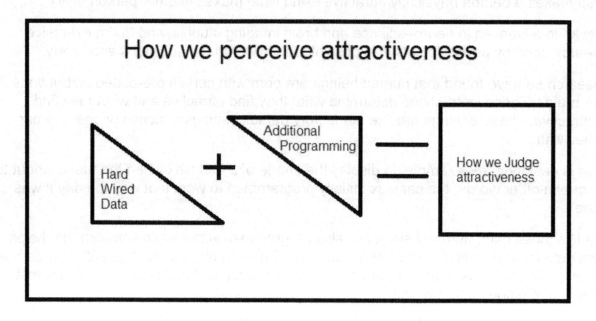

The Attraction Puzzle

Why do certain people become attracted to certain facial features and why do others find the same facial features repulsive?

As I mentioned earlier, there are universal features that determine physical attractiveness, but, if this is the case, why don't all people fall for the same exact person?

Moreover, why can you find someone attractive yet prefer to be with someone else because the first is not your type?

Why would you agree with your friend that a certain person who has round facial features is attractive, yet you tell him that round features aren't your type!

Why do we have types when it comes to judging physical attractiveness?

After all, if we were born with a certain software that can help us identify beautiful faces, then we must all be attracted to the same physical features, right?

No, that's not the case, and here is why...

Each one of us develops certain needs as a result of going through certain life experiences. These unmet needs determine what our desired partner should look like.

For example, if a girl felt that her past relationship partner wasn't good enough because he refused to bear responsibility, she will always look for men who are more manly and masculine.

Based on this experience, this female might only be attracted to men who look more masculine or those who have masculine facial features.

Whilst all women are biologically designed to look for such masculine men, this woman in particular will put more weight on these masculine features.

Now compare this to a woman who was abused by an aggressive man and who suffered from a horrible experience. In such a case, this woman might avoid men with facial features that indicate the presence of aggression. In other words, this woman might be attracted to men who have more feminine features!

So the experiences we go through teach us that certain people are good for us and certain ones are bad, and this is one reason why people start developing 'types'.

How People Associate Personality Traits with Physical Looks

Now the question is, why do some people dislike certain facial features even if they don't indicate the presence of bad personality traits?

Why would a man dislike women with round facial features and prefer ones with straight features?

The answer to these questions lies in the associations a man has made between those facial features and some personality traits during his past. If a man was taught that fat people are lazy, or if his beliefs state that people with sharp features are more active, then he will unconsciously be repelled by any woman who has round facial features.

Sometimes, the problem lies in the 'associations' a person has formed, and not the facial features themselves. This is how your mind works. The mind forms 'associations' all the time and thus connects unrelated things to each other. Here is a popular example of such associations: A man who fears loss of control might find himself afraid of the dark as well.

While he might believe that he fears the dark because of ghosts, the truth is that he fears it because he fears 'loss of control'.

A woman who always feels jealous of her friends might start fearing cats. Again, the woman's subconscious mind connects two unrelated things (women and cats) and resulted in triggering unpleasant emotions whenever the latter object is encountered.

A man who is obsessed about losing his social status might develop an obsessive compulsive disorder which causes him to check his car door is lock every now and then. The fear of losing his social status is unconsciously associated with the fear of losing his car.

So, before you can begin to understand why a person won't like certain facial features, you need to know two things:

- ⅄ What his unmet needs are (what desires he is trying to fulfil).

- ⅄ How his subconscious connects certain objects together.

A man who hasn't learned to associate laziness with round features will still be attracted to a woman with round features even if he hates laziness.

So, the key to understanding the way people perceive physical features is to understand how their minds connect unrelated objects together.

Now does this ring any bells?

Have you been rejected because of your looks before?

The good news, as you may now begin to understand, is that the problem might not be with your looks at all, but rather with the way a person associates your looks with certain personality traits.

A Case Study

When Tim was young he believed he was a helpless child. The best solution he had for the problems he used to face was to cry. As the years passed, Tim started resenting his helplessness and as a result, he decided to be the exact opposite.

A person's psychological goals and unmet needs are developed as a result of the childhood experiences they go through, as you will see later in this book. In Tim's case, no longer being helpless was his ultimate goal.

Tim also started to dislike helpless people automatically. And another factor came into play and shaped the way Tim thought; the culture he was raised in taught him that obese people are helpless. Therefore, Tim would label any obese person as being a 'helpless person'.

Tim also never understood why he was only attracted to women who had sharp facial features and not round ones.

This is because Tim's subconscious mind associated round objects with obesity and that's why round facial features used to turn him off. Of course, Tim never understood what was going on because everything happened on an unconscious level.

It's clear that Tim was turned off by round facial features just because he used to feel helpless as a child!

The subconscious mind just connects objects together even if they seemed completely unrelated. That's also why you sometimes see symbols in your dreams that represent real-life objects.

Your subconscious mind works using symbols and that's why it might connect certain facial features with certain personality traits without you noticing.

This brings us to a very important point. If you were rejected because of your looks, then you must bear in mind that the person who rejected you might have done it because of their own psychological make-up and not because you are ugly.

When you get to know how people see others and why they develop certain preferences for physical beauty you will come to realize that many good-looking people can actually be rejected for their looks!

People are attracted to what they Lack

I get many emails from people who tell me they are unhappy with their looks because they dislike one of their facial features. Many people also tell me they don't like the shape of their nose and that they believe others won't like them because their nose doesn't look attractive.

The one important fact those people have missed is that most people are concerned about the things they lack the most.

If a man drives a Ferrari but has recently spent more than one month waiting for it to be fixed, then he might actually start envying the guy who drives an average car which can be fixed in a day or two.

People always look for the things they lack. While you might be concerned about the shape of your nose, the people who are important to you might be focusing on your healthy body, beautiful hair, or your self-confidence.

Each person sees the world from a different angle and that's why the things that concern you the most aren't necessarily the things that concern others.

When someone meets a new person they quickly compare themselves to them by looking for the traits that the other person has and that they lack. That's why in most cases people end up feeling inferior to each other!

For example, Joe and Jack met for the first time in their lives. Joe was concerned he was shorter than Jack and was afraid Jack believed he was short and weak!

Jack on the other hand had a bigger belly, and he was afraid that Joe believed he was fat.

Therefore, both Joe and Jack did not feel confident around each other! Had any one of them known what the other was thinking, he would have felt more confident.

The people around you are not perfect, even the ones who seem perfect. When you judge the beauty of others, you will usually do it according to your own standards and that's why you might believe that an average person has superior beauty.

It's all about the lens you use. Now, you might be wondering how a person you judged, judges his own attractiveness?

As you will see later in this book, the media today strongly affects the way people see themselves. Because the media always portrays people who have very rare genes and who are much less likely to exist on this planet, people lose their self-confidence when they compare themselves to those people.

Even beautiful people never manage to get away from these deadly comparisons and they end up disliking their looks.

The people around you also think the same and they always compare themselves to these impossible standards and that's why you must rest assured when being around anybody.

While you might be intimidated by the beauty of an attractive person, this person could also be feeling unattractive because of the impossible standards she compares herself with on a regular basis.

In short, while the media has done a bad job in advertising these impossible standards, it still gives you the chance to feel confident around others once you know how they think.

Why do some People Find Themselves Attractive and Others don't?

Why can a person with average beauty believe he is very attractive, and why can a beautiful person think she is not desirable?

Many people feel unattractive even though they are good-looking. To understand how this strange phenomenon happens, you need to understand how a person judges his own attractiveness.

The way a person judges his own attractiveness is based on two things:

- ⋏ His beliefs about how attraction happens.

- ⋏ His resources and his physical features.

Let's assume that a rich, popular, and intelligent man has an averagely attractive face. If that man believes that facial attraction is the most important factor for attracting women, then he might feel unattractive even though he possesses some traits that can attract most women, as you will understand later in the book.

On the other hand, if that man understands that many women can favour personality, resources, and wealth over physical looks, then he will feel very attractive.

So the key point is how the person believes others judge attractiveness. That's why knowing more about the psychology of attraction can help a lot of people who think that they are not attractive to feel good about themselves.

You might be feeling unattractive now because you have not understood the process of attraction correctly! Many people who believe they are not attractive change their ideas about their own attractiveness completely after they get to know how others see them.

For example; if a woman doesn't like her nose because it's a little too big, and who at the same time has a low waist to hip ratio and feminine facial features, then she might not feel that she is attractive.

The reason this woman believes she is not attractive is because of the false belief she has about how the looks of the nose can affect attractiveness perception.

Once this woman understands that men judge the overall attractiveness of women without spending much time analysing each feature on its own, then she will feel more attractive.

Of course, a beautiful nose shape is desirable, but if your overall looks are good then you will be labelled attractive by most men with no regard to the shape of your nose.

In other words, a correct understanding of attraction psychology can make you feel much more attractive.

Unmet Needs in Psychology

In psychology, the term 'unmet needs' refers to the needs a person hasn't managed to satisfy yet.

Just as there are physical needs such as the need to eat or the need to sleep, there are psychological needs that people must satisfy in order to feel good.

When people fail to satisfy their important unmet needs they become depressed, and when people manage to fulfil their unmet needs they experience true happiness.

Unmet needs might also result in unhealthy addictions. Many of the substance abusers and many of those who are addicted to bad habits are just trying to satisfy an important unmet need that they haven't managed to satisfy otherwise.

Unmet needs are developed as a result of the life experiences we go through. If a child was raised in a family that suffered from financial problems and if the child was ambitious, then he will certainly develop the need to become rich. Up until that person becomes rich, he will live with his unmet need and as a result:

⚑   He will become motivated whenever he finds a way that can make him rich and thus satisfy his unmet need.

⚑   He will become indifferent if he doesn't believe that the tasks he is undertaking will make him rich.

⚑   He will become depressed if he loses his money on the stock market. Depression is nothing more than an emotion you get when your mind discovers that the road to satisfying your unmet needs is blocked.

As you can see, all of your emotions can be perfectly understood in the light of 'unmet needs'.

Many people try to define happiness by talking about it from their own perspective. This is a catastrophic mistake. Happiness can only be understood in the light of the unmet needs of each person on an individual basis.

If I suffer from financial insecurity (an unmet need for becoming rich), then certainly money can make me happy. If another person doesn't have this unmet need, then money won't mean anything to him.

Addiction is 99% psychological. If a person has a certain unmet need that he wishes to satisfy, he might find himself having a certain bad habit without realizing he is doing it to satisfy that unmet need.

For example, many people become addicted to drugs in order to escape from their problems and in order to feel good about themselves. The unmet needs they are suffering from make their life unbearable and that's why they decided to become addicted to escape from their unsatisfied unmet needs. Had they managed to satisfy their unmet needs, they wouldn't have needed drugs to feel good.

Sometimes, a person gets into a relationship just to satisfy an unmet need. If a girl was raised by a distant father, she might develop an unmet need for being taken care of and that's why she might be attracted to the first guy who takes care of her, provided that he matches her other criteria.

If a guy lacks self-confidence (unmet need), he might be attracted to the first girl who makes him feel good about himself, if she meets his basic criteria.

Now this brings us to a very important point. Sometimes, you might get rejected just because of an unmet need that the person you are after has, and not because there is anything wrong with you.

If a guy was rejected by a blonde female long ago, he might develop an unmet need to be with a blonde female. Now this guy can reject a good-looking brunette just because she can't help him satisfy his important unmet need.

While the guy will still acknowledge that the brunette is beautiful, he will still believe she is not his type without actually knowing why.

Were you rejected earlier? The problem might be with the unmet needs of the person who rejected you earlier, and not with you.

Attractiveness and Culture

Does culture affect attractiveness?

Are there universal standards for beauty or is there a variation in such standards across different cultures?

Long ago a tan was completely unattractive as it usually indicated that the person had to work outdoors most of the time and was not rich enough to work in an office. These days the opposite is true because of a change in culture. Nowadays, a tan usually indicates that the person is wealthy enough to think about getting tanned and to travel somewhere hot, which can help him get tanned.

There is no doubt that culture affects perceived attractiveness, but the important question is, is there a universal culture that makes beauty standards the same all over the world?

Research has shown that even if there are slight variations in preference among people, there are still general beauty standards everyone agrees on across all cultures.

Because of globalization and the widespread use of the Internet and advances in the telecommunications industry, Western culture has managed to promote beauty standards to the whole world and to almost every culture.

Isolated tribes that have their own culture and are not exposed to any other cultures still have their own unique beauty standards and their unique definition for attractiveness. This shows that if each culture was isolated from the others, attractiveness standards would be completely different from one culture to another.

While most of the biologically hardwired instructions for determining personal attractiveness will still be the same across all cultures, a person's culture will program the programmable part of his brain and affect the way he perceives physical attractiveness. Culture isn't the only thing that determines attractiveness because each person has his own learned attractiveness standards.

For example, if a person lives in a culture that has taught him to believe that slim women are attractive, then the person might be attracted to slim women, but at the same time he will add his own preferences in order to be able to choose between many of the slim women he knows.

The Differences between Men and Women

How Men and Women Perceive Physical Attractiveness

Attractiveness is multi-dimensional. There are many domains across which attraction can happen, and not just the physical attraction domain. All studies, without exception, have shown that men put a higher weight on physical looks than women.

Of course, men look for other traits apart from physical attraction, but in most cases physical looks will have the highest priority when a man judges a woman's attractiveness.

The reason I mention this fact after the introduction I gave in the first few pages is not to disappoint you because you now know exactly what the term 'physically attractive' means. When I use the words 'physically attractive', I not am referring to the models you see on TV, but I am referring to a certain combination of physical features a certain person will find attractive based on his culture, past experience, unmet needs, and all the other factors that contribute to the way he judges physical attraction.

Many women are disappointed when they know that most men care about physical looks so much because they never attempt to understand what physical attraction means.

There is another very good piece of news I have for you. There are many things a woman can do in order to appear more attractive to men, even if she isn't very attractive. I will talk about this later in this book, but for now I will continue to explain how both sexes perceive attractiveness.

A man can become attracted to a woman and even decide to be with her as soon as he sees her, while a woman usually needs more than one thing to be present before she starts to become attracted to a man.

There is a saying that I like that explains how both sexes perceive attractiveness. 'Women are like ovens, whilst men are like lighters. A man needs a few seconds to heat, just like a lighter., while a woman needs some time to reach a high temperature, just like an oven'.

This is why women take more time to develop strong emotions towards men:

When judging attractiveness, women respond to different cues across many domains. Women are attracted to a man's resources, his personality, the way he treats others, and many other things. Women are more complex because they need to look for many cues together before they can decide whether they are attracted to a man or not.

That's why most women need some time before they can make up their mind about being with a man. A man, on the other hand, can make this decision almost instantly.

Because women have to invest much more emotional and physical effort to raise their offspring, they were designed to be more selective when picking a mating partner.

I once came across an online group on Facebook which allowed people to post anonymous messages about their crushes.

While most men focused on the physical attractiveness of women, many of the women wrote messages that described the way a man would interact with others or ones that outlined his good personality traits such as: 'He has a lot of friends', 'people love him', 'he seems so kind', and 'I always see him reading'.

Men are simple. They get turned on by any woman who looks healthy and fertile. The hour-glass body shape, the full lips, the symmetry of the face, and the low waist to hip ratio are all indicators of the presence of a good supply of the female hormone that promotes fertility. A small nose, large eyes, and a small chin are also indicators of a good supply of female hormones.

A man can make up his mind about being with a certain woman at first glance, and as superficial as this seems to be, still it's considered a biological fact.

This doesn't mean that men can choose life partners just because a woman looks good. It means that men will at least get aroused by women who are physically attractive even if they know nothing else about them. Men also collect signals from different domains and assess a woman's attractiveness based on them, but for most men physical attractiveness will be the number one priority.

Women, on the other hand, are more complicated; yes they do care about looks, but the way they are made prevents them from being turned on unless the man meets certain important criteria they are looking for.

I once read a statement that explains it all; 'Men need a place to have sex, women need a reason!'

Research has found that women don't get aroused before a man meets the important subconscious criteria they are looking for. In other words, a woman can become turned on after she realizes that a certain man can provide her with security, protection, or whatever she is looking for.

This is why there is no effective drug like Viagra to enhance sexual performance for women. It's because a woman's mind gets involved and prevents her from being turned on if the wrong man is present.

This is also another cause of sexual problems that happen between men and women after marriage. If a woman loses respect for her man or feels he is not man enough, she might not experience any arousal during the sexual process.

Because many men don't understand these facts, they quickly lose their self esteem as soon as a woman rejects them. These men assume women think the same way they do, and that's why they start believing they are physically unattractive if they got rejected, forgetting that women need some time to look for other important traits apart from physical attractiveness.

Apart from physical attraction, women are attracted to dominant men, alpha males, and bad boys.

Women are also attracted to resourceful men and ambitious ones. An expensive watch can attract a woman to a man the same way a woman's looks can attract a man. It's not that women are materialistic, it's just that women are biologically wired to seek the most resourceful men.

Many men who have average looks get out of the game too early because they believe women will not be attracted to them. The good news is, even if a woman doesn't find you attractive, she can still find you sexually attractive after she gets to know more about your personality traits.

When it comes to judging the attractiveness of men, women put weight on many factors such power, wealth, and dominance as well as physical attraction.

One experiment in particular was carried out where two men were photographed. One man was wearing a Burger King uniform and the other was wearing an expensive looking suit accompanied with a Rolex watch.

The first group of women shown the pictures of the two men were asked to rate them, and the second group of women were shown the same pictures after the two men switched their uniforms.

Most women didn't want to date the man with the Burger King uniform and the majority preferred the man wearing the expensive suit.

This study and many others prove the same thing; status and resources can compensate for a man's physical beauty. Men, on the other hand, don't care much about a woman's resources and are more motivated by physical beauty than women.

Men are not superficial, but their brains were wired in such a way that visual cues attract them the most. Both men and women care about physical looks, but for most men, if not all, physical looks come top of the list.

Men were created in such a way that they are attracted to healthy and fertile women. In other words, if men pick up certain cues that show that a certain woman is capable of bearing healthy offspring, he will be attracted to her.

Brain scanning studies have also shown something very interesting. For the brains of men who were shown pictures of their lovers, it was found that men were most stimulated by visual stimuli. However, when the same study was carried out on women, it was found that the most active areas in their brain at the time of stimulation were the areas of memory recall.

In other words, a woman looks back into her memory to fetch certain data about a man in order to find him attractive. Scientists have stated that this data is the man's personality, or it could be his resources.

In other words, men need to access the visual areas of their brain in order to assess the attractiveness of a woman, while women need to access their memory bank to determine the attractiveness of a man.

To summarize all this, I find nothing better than this picture which I found online. it explains the whole story in a second:

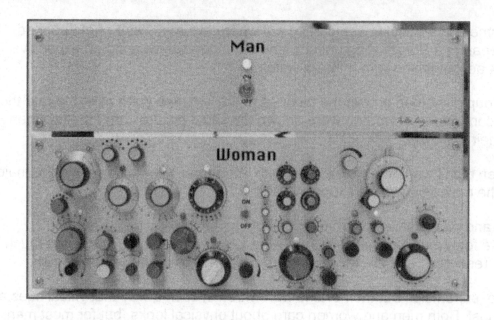

Why Women Pay More Attention to Detail

Now the question is: why do women pay more attention to detail than men when it comes to choosing a partner?

A man can have sex with a woman once and face no consequences, but a woman might become pregnant, give birth, and find herself responsible for a child who needs to be taken care of.

Because women invest more than men in relationships, and because they might suffer from greater consequences, they tend to be pickier than men when choosing a life partner.

When a human being develops a certain psychological need his behavior usually changes to help him satisfy this need. Because women need to find the right man they automatically find themselves drawn to more specific details when they evaluate men.

A typical woman might change her idea about a man when she sees him playing with a little child, but a typical man will usually ignore such a detail.

That's another reason why women tend to find men with dogs more attractive. It's because they believe that these men are more responsible and are better able to take care of a child.

Financial Independence and Looks Preferences

Another study has shown that women tend to find men more physically attractive if they earn a higher income. Here is how the study was carried out:

Pictures of men were shown to women and they were asked to rate their physical attractiveness.

After the ratings were recorded, the men's incomes were written beside the pictures and the women were asked to rate them again. It was found that the men who earned a high income became more physically attractive to the women.

It's not that the women chose the men who earned a higher income with their minds, but it actually happened that those women started perceiving the physical attractiveness of these men differently after they found out about their incomes.

Another interesting study has shown that women who are financially independent care more about looks. From a biological point of view, women need a man who can provide her with resources because they want to feel secure, but when a woman becomes self-reliant as a result of having a great career or good financial resources, she tends to ignore men's resources and look for physical beauty.

This doesn't mean that every woman who is financially independent will care about the man's looks the most, it means that some of those women might prefer physical looks over resources since they don't need their resources that much.

Why do Men Care about Looks more than Women do?

I am sure you have never heard a man saying "I like her because she is the healthiest and most fertile woman I have ever seen." Simply because, most men don't know how their brains work.

Men are just attracted to certain features that indicate the presence of enough supply of the female hormone. This is the way God ensured a man will have the largest number of offspring, because a woman with the best health and highest female hormonal levels will be the most fertile woman.

Men are attracted to women with a low waist to hip ratio, full lips, symmetrical faces, large eyes, small chins, and feminine facial features in general.

But what about a woman's weight?

Some recent studies have shown that men's preference for slim women is just a cultural phenomenon. They back up their research with evidence that some isolated tribes still prefer heavy women over slimmer ones.

One study found that throughout history men have changed their preferences about a woman's weight, but they have always retained the low waist to hip ratio requirement.

Another theory states that men are attracted to heavy women in some cultures where food is scarce, and to slim women where there is plenty of food. In the first case men are attracted to those women because they come from wealthy families, while in the second case they are attracted to those women because they are healthier than others.

In other words, a woman's weight is one of the things men learned to judge as a result of their learning capacity. The media, with the way it portrays slim models, has taught men to prefer them over heavier ones.

Do Men only Care about Looks?

Yes, men do care about looks to a great extent. Physical beauty in most cases resides at the top of every man's wish list. But have you ever asked yourself the question, what is meant by physical beauty??

- **1) The perception of physical beauty changes from one man to another:**
  People perceive physical attractiveness differently even if it seems that there are

universally agreed upon beauty standards. In other words, you could believe you have average looks while another person believes you are very beautiful.

- **2) More than just the face:** Men don't consider a woman attractive when all of her features are perfect, but they find a woman attractive when she has one or two attractive features. In order words, if your body is fit then you will still be found attractive even if you dislike your facial features! The great thing about your body weight is that it's completely under your control.

- **3) Relativity and attractiveness:** Most women consider themselves unattractive because they compare themselves to the celebrities they see on TV, forgetting that attractiveness perceptions change according to the available options. This means that men won't compare you to TV celebrities unless many of them live in a nearby block. People judge attractiveness based on the available options, and as a result a person of average attractiveness can still be found very attractive

- **4) Clothes and attractiveness:** Men find women who wear attractive clothes much more attractive than other women who wear normal clothes. Again a man can find you attractive just because you appear to be from a good social class.

The conclusion is: Men care about looks but there are many other factors that could change the way they see you.

Men judge the overall attractiveness of women based on many cues and not just her facial features. If the shape of your nose is not perfect or if you dislike something about your face then remind yourself that many other parameters can alter your overall attractiveness.

The way you talk, the way you walk, the clothes you choose and so many other factors that aren't related to your looks can still affect your physical attractiveness in the eyes of men.

What can a Woman do to Attract a Man?

Men of course do care about other factors in addition to physical looks even if they put a high weight on physical looks. The female's personality, the way she dresses and her feminine attitude are all factors that can add to the attractiveness of a woman who has average looks.

Women should care about their looks, exercise often, and should stay fit if they want to increase their chances of attracting men. In some cultures, women ignore their looks more than others and then state that personality is everything.

While this may sound like a wise saying, it's completely against the biology of a human male. Many women who don't want to make more of an effort to become fit or who can't exert more control over their appetite, run to those philosophies in order to feel good about themselves.

The "don't judge a book by its cover" saying may seem very wise, but when it comes to real life, this saying has no place. Lots of studies have been carried out to find out how physical attractiveness affects the way both males and females deal with a person.

Here are some of the findings they came up with:

- Taller men earn more than shorter men.

- Physical beauty increases the chance of getting a job.

- Babies gaze more at attractive faces.

- Mothers give more attention to more attractive babies.

- Teachers believe attractive students are more intelligent.

Each point outlined above is a finding by a concrete study that was carried out by experts. In other words, physical attraction matters a lot to both males and females.

Even if you are an average-looking woman living a healthy lifestyle and having a healthy body, these factors will give you a superior advantage over other women who don't do the same.

In fact, health and physical beauty are strongly interconnected. You can hardly get one without getting the other. If you focus on your health and weight then you will surely become much more attractive.

And as I mentioned earlier, physical attractiveness perception differs from one person to another. This means that what one man finds unattractive, can still be found attractive by another man. So never worry, there will always be a man out there who thinks that you are attractive.

Body Shape and Attraction

Men are attracted to women who have a low waist to hip ratio. The optimum waist to hip ratio that has been found to be attractive by most men is 0.8.

It has also been found that women who have a waist to hip ratio that is close to the ideal are more fertile. This low waist to hip ratio indicates the presence of a good amount of female hormones and as a result those women have higher chances of conceiving.

Again, God designed men in such a way that they are attracted to women who are most fertile in order to help human beings have more offspring.

The good news I have for women here is that many men can sacrifice facial attractiveness for a good-looking body. While it's very hard to change physical looks, body shape can still be changed with a certain workout routine and good discipline.

Bear in mind, however, that the waist to hip ratio has nothing to do with body weight. As I mentioned earlier, the way men judge the female body has been found to be culturally influenced. In earlier days, heavy women were found to be more attractive to men. This can be easily guessed from early status and poems that idolized heavy women.

Women on the other hand are attracted to men with v-shaped bodies. Broad shoulders and a narrow waist both contribute to the v-shaped torso of a man which attracts women.

Even though women put less weight on physical looks, it has been found that they prefer men with v-shaped bodies provided all the other factors are constant. It has also been found that women prefer muscular men, but not men who are overly muscular.

Women are biologically wired to feel the need for security and protection, and that's why any cue that can send an indirect message to the subconscious mind of a woman to make her feel secure, will attract her to men.

Physical Height and Attraction

Most women prefer to date taller men. Again, this happens because physical height unconsciously targets the need for security most women have.

Studies have shown that taller men get more dates and even earn more money throughout their lives.

The good news I have for shorter men is that if you make a woman feel secure by targeting any of the other aspects she is attracted to, you won't have to worry much about your height.

Dominance, strong personality, courage, wealth, self-confidence, and ambition are all things that can compensate for the physical height of a man (see next section).

Men on the other hand prefer to date women who are shorter than them. This gives the man the unconscious feeling that he is in control. Most men will be intimated by taller women and some of them may prefer not to approach them.

Studies have also shown that men prefer women who have a longer lower body, or in other words, longer legs. Again, each item in the attraction puzzle has a slight impact on the overall attractiveness of a person, but when they are all put together they greatly impact the attractiveness of a person.

Another study has found that women prefer taller men and not tall men. This is good news for shorter men because even if a man is not tall compared to his friends, he will still have a good chance If he is taller than the woman he is targeting.

Do Short Men have any Chance?

So the question is, do short men have any chance?
Yes they certainly Do!

If a short man manages to satisfy the unconscious need for protection a woman has, then there is a great chance that she won't be concerned about his physical height.

This need for protection can be satisfied using the following methods:

- **Being more confident & dominant:** When the man becomes more confident and dominant the woman will automatically feel secure around him even if he isn't tall.

- **Being more resourceful:** The more skilled the man is, the higher a man's status and the more resources he possesses, the more the woman will feel safe around him and the more they will be attracted to him.

The subconscious mind of a woman can receive the same reassuring message through different channels, and that's why even if your height is not ideal you can still have a good chance of attracting women.

Physical height and status

The higher a man's status, the taller he appears to be! Studies have shown that many women can sacrifice physical appearance in exchange for higher status.

If you are a man then know that physical appearance might not matter much when it comes to assessing your overall attractiveness.

This doesn't mean that looks aren't important for women. Women measure the attractiveness of a man based on many cues across multiple domains, and the physical attractiveness of a man is just one of the elements a woman depends upon to assess the overall attractiveness of a man.

In short, you do have a chance even if you are shorter than your peers.

Other Qualities Besides Looks

When the word "attractive" is mentioned, most people come to think of physical looks. Recent studies have shown that physical looks are only one of the elements involved in the attraction puzzle! This means there are many other factors apart from your physical looks that determine your overall attractiveness.

The way you talk, what you do, your tone of voice, your personality, your status, sense of humour, and many other factors can affect the way people perceive your physical attractiveness to a great extent.

In other words, when I say that people prefer to date attractive people, I am actually referring to the other "overall attractiveness" of a person, and not just his physical appearance. Each time physical attractiveness is mentioned in this book, bear in mind that physical appearance is only a fraction of your perceived physical attractiveness.

In this section I will be talking about many factors that affect your level of attractiveness.

The Man who has the Resources

Just as men are biologically wired to look for healthy and fertile women, women are biologically wired to look for resourceful men to feel safe and secure. They also want protection and to ensure a good future for their offspring. This happens on an unconscious level, and as a result most women will be attracted to resourceful men provided that all the other variables are constant.

Of course, money is the most powerful resource a man can have, but this does not mean that you can't attract women if you don't have it.

Women aren't attracted to rich men and that's it, they also are attracted to men who might become rich one day. This means that an ambitious man might have the same chance as a rich man.

Some other factors give woman indications of the presence of resources. The way a man is dressed, the way he talks about the future and his level of education are all factors that can show the woman that this man might become rich one day.

This is also why women might take notice of a man's watch, his shoes, and his car. These things give them an indication of the level of resources he can provide them with.

Some people say that money only attracts gold diggers, but this is a common misconception. A gold digger is a woman who will go for the rich man even if she doesn't like anything else about him, while another woman will only go for the resourceful man because she likes other things about him and not just his money or resources.

If you are not rich, don't worry. Men can compensate for the lack of money by using ambition. If you prove to the woman you are very ambitious, she will assume that you will become rich one day and so she will overlook your lack of resources.

What about Women who Say they don't Think that Way?

While there might be a few women out there who think differently, still the majority of women will say they don't think that way. It's not that they want to lie, they are not aware of the way their minds work.

Those women might fantasize about certain men, but as soon as the resourceful male gets into the game, their calculations differ and they will go for him.

In short, money attracts women because looking for resourceful men is part of their biological make-up. Forget about what a women might say and just watch her actions.

Does our Personality Affect our Level of Attractiveness?

Studies have shown that attractiveness perception changes when we get to know a person better.

Do you remember how your perception of attractiveness of people changed during high school or college days? I am sure you found some people attractive after spending more time with them even though you didn't find them attractive during your first encounter.

A study has shown that people start to see others differently when they discover some of their personality traits.

When was the last time you saw a movie where the hero wasn't that attractive? Do you remember how you felt when you first saw a particular movie hero? Try to recall your feelings towards him at the end of the movie and you will discover that you have changed your opinion about his physical attractiveness completely.

If watching a person do good deeds for two hours can change attractiveness perception, what can a six-month friendship with a person do?

Certainly, if during that period the person displays desirable traits, then he will appear much more physically attractive!

We all have certain standards that we use to asses people's attractiveness, but when we spend time with someone with desirable traits we start to sacrifice some of these standards.

It's as if our subconscious minds replace some of the physical traits of that person with some of his good personality traits.

It has also been found that people can change their attractiveness perception a few seconds after a person starts talking! Sometimes, the first impression a person forms of another is changed as soon as the latter speaks.

Another study has found that a simple action such as a friendly smile can affect the attractiveness perception of people. If a smile does this, what can a good trait such as courage do?

You don't have to look like movie heroes to leave a good impression because just as you can see, people can see you differently based on your actions and behaviour

While these facts are applicable to both men and women, it has been found that a woman is more likely to change her perception of physical attractiveness of a man after he displays great personality traits.

Just as I said earlier, physical looks are only one item in the attraction puzzle. The more you know about this attraction puzzle the more you will be able to take advantage of such facts and the more attractive you will appear to be.

Smiling and Physical Attraction

A recent study has shown that women rate happy men or men who smile often as less attractive than men who look proud and arrogant!

At the first instance, this might seem like a fact that contradicts what previous research has come up with. We have all heard that a sense of humour makes a person much more attractive, so how can a smile make someone less attractive?

The same study showed that men found women who smile to be more attractive than women who looked proud. The reason the perception of the smile differed from men to women is that smiling can be interpreted as a sign of submission, and because men prefer women who smile more attractive.

Women, on the other hand, prefer men with higher power and status. This is why a man with a proud and arrogant look appears much more attractive to women.

Men who display an "angry look" appear more dominant and in control; two traits that women always look for in men.

It was found that men who joke in a proud or cocky way appear much more attractive to women than other men.

Women find proud-looking men more attractive, yet at the same time they want a man who has a good sense of humour, which is why combining both arrogance and a sense of humour brings the best results.

If you are a woman, you will appear more attractive if you smile more often, while if you are a man, a proud look will give you a much more attractive look.

However, there is an exception to this rule. Many women out there don't have enough self-esteem, and that's why an angry look or an unfriendly approach might scare them. In such a case, a smile can be used to comfort these women.

If you are a man, smile less often during the first meeting or the first encounter, but later on, after you make sure you have displayed the right status, you can smile more often.

If you are a woman then smile more often and men will find you more attractive. In another study, women who had a proud look were rated as the least attractive by most men. It seems that this proud look represents a challenge to the man's dominance and ego and that's why it turns men off.

Just as you will see in the next few pages, women prefer bad boys or dangerous men.

This also adds more weight to the fact that smiling less often can make a man much more attractive. The less a man smiles, the more he looks like a dangerous bad boy, which is the typical type that attracts most women.

Why being 'Cocky' Attracts Women

No one likes arrogant people, especially when they treat us badly, but what about people who are cocky in a funny way?

When a woman meets a potential partner, she will quickly asses his ability to provide security and protection. Women were designed in this way so that they pick the man who can take care of a family the most.

Women pick up the messages men send through all possible channels. If a man is found to be rich or ambitious, a woman will believe that he can be a good protector.

If a man is found to be tall, a woman might believe that he is a good protector as well.

If a man is found to be confident and a natural leader, a woman will also assume he can provide protection.

Is it becoming clear now?

A confident man will most likely be able to take good care of the family, at least that's how women were designed to think. That's why women love cocky men.

If a person is cocky but distant and unfriendly, people will automatically hate him. No one wants to feel rejected or unloved, and that's why the cocky but funny man is considered very attractive to women.

Do Women Care about Looks?

This question confuses many guys because of the presence of contradicting facts everywhere. When guys read articles or hear information explaining what attracts women to men, they find financial resources, personality, and ambition at top of the list. However, when they deal with women, they find them chasing good-looking guys and that's it!

So how can this mystery be explained? I said earlier in the book that women are attracted to the most resourceful men because of their need for protection and their desire to have a man who can take care of his offspring. This is a hardwired biological drive in women.

On the other hand, you may find women talking about how amazing a certain man looks, and you find others madly in love with movie heroes just because they look good. What's going on in here?

Here is the explanation:

Most women care about looks but not as much as men do except for those who have low self-esteem. In such a case, they want to prove they can get a good-looking man.

Most women will be attracted to a resourceful man more than they are attracted to a good-looking man, but because looks are the first thing to be noticed many women chase attractive men just because they don't recognize resourceful ones.

In other words, if a handsome man and an average- looking man with high status went to a public place, the handsome man would catch the attention of a women first. However, if the high status man managed to communicate his status, most women would be drawn to him.

Women chase attractive men because average-looking men don't market their status and resources well. Of course, it's much easier for the attractive man to get initial interest, simply because his best is written on his face.

As for the resourceful man, his chances might be better if he managed to demonstrate his status in a good way.

Women are attracted to resourceful men, confident ones and "Alpha Males." A resourceful man isn't necessarily the one who has the money, but he can be the one who has the resources that can help him make money one day

An average-looking man must market these traits correctly in order to realize his full potential or else the woman will make the comparison based on what she can see (looks), and he will lose the comparison.

In brief, women do care about looks, but there are other things that they care about, and in most cases those other things carry more weight than looks. However, when a woman can see nothing but looks, because of poor marketing strategies that the average-looking man uses, then the best-looking man will win.

Attraction, Uncertainty and Perceived Value

In one study, women were shown profile pictures of men on Facebook and were told that those men had rated their attractiveness earlier.

One group of women were told that the men rated them as very attractive. The second group of women were told that the men rated them as attractive on an average basis, while the third group were told that the men either gave them average or very attractive ratings.

Here is what happened. The participants who were uncertain about the ratings became more attached to the men who rated them than those who were certain.

In other words, uncertainty about a person's intentions makes him much more attractive.

This is because our minds were designed to get rid of completed tasks because they are no longer useful. If you want to refuel your car then most probably you will keep thinking about that task until you do it.

Once you have completed this task, you are less likely to think about it again. Exactly the same goes for attraction. When you are certain that a person likes you, you won't think about him as often as you would have thought about him if you were uncertain about his intentions.

This is also why confusing people works like magic. When a person becomes uncertain whether you like him or not then there is a very big possibility that he will think about you more often. This is one reason why nice guys turn women off! They are just too predictable to the extent that they give women no room to think about them.

But there is a very important question that still needs an answer.

Why is it that some people aren't affected, even when they are uncertain about your emotions?

I am sure you tried confusing someone before only to discover that he is completely uninterested in you. Here is why it happens:

Every person is attracted to the people who satisfy his important subconscious criteria (a set of conditions that were formed as a result of that person's past experiences).

Now, if you satisfy some subconscious criteria of that particular person and then you begin confusing him, then most probably, he will start thinking about you more often and he might fall in love with you.

In other words, a person won't bother to know your real intentions if you aren't that valuable to him. That's why the first step you should take when attempting to attract a person is to become more valuable to him by satisfying his subconscious criteria.

Once you do this, you can move on to step two, which is confusing him. This will increase the chance of making this person fall for you ten times over or even more.

Most people make the mistake of trying to confuse the person right away without impressing him first, and that's why their targets ignore their attempts. If you have rated a person as five out of ten, then most probably you wont think much about him if you are unsure of his intentions.

Compare this to a nine who is treating you in a mysterious way. Most probably, you will keep thinking about him all day just to work out whether he likes you or not.

Even if you aren't interested in that person, you will still think about him because the reward of making sure he likes you will be a good one.

Every person will get a boost in self-confidence if he knows that an attractive person likes him. That's why people do this "over thinking."

Now, the good news is that the more a person thinks about you, the more he will become attached to you even if he wasn't interested in you in the beginning.

Attraction and Relationship with Parents

Studies have shown that men prefer to be with younger women, while women prefer to be with older men. Because women want to feel safe and secure, they feel more comfortable around mature, older men.

Men, on the other hand, prefer women who are younger because a young age is a good indicator of a woman's health.

One interesting study has attempted to find out why certain kinds of women prefer certain ages in men. The study found that if the age difference between the girl and her father is big then she might become attracted to older men.

Note that this won't happen unless the girl likes her father and thinks of him as a role model. The better the relationship between a girl and her father, the more likely she will be looking for someone who looks like him when choosing a life partner.

The same goes for men. The better the relationship between a man and his mother, the more likely it is he is going to look for a woman who resembles her.

Note that this selection process happens on the unconscious level based on the signals the unconscious mind notices. For example, you will rarely find a woman who says that she likes a man because he reminds her of her father. Instead, her subconscious mind will notice some similarities between that man and the parent.

These similarities could take many forms such as:

- Certain facial features.
- The way he talks.
- The way he walks or his body language.
- His tone of voice.
- His opinions or beliefs about life.

However, if the relationship with the opposite sex parent isn't good, the opposite might happen. A girl might not fall for the man who reminds her of her abusive father, even if that man wasn't abusive.

Now you might be asking yourself, why do some people always fall for their abusers?

The answer is simple. Some people prefer to avoid what happened in the past and to go on with a fresh start and that's why they will always repel those who remind them of their abusers. Other people want to be victorious over their abuser, so they are attracted to the people who look like him just because this gives them another chance to win!

If a father was always absent and his daughter was subsequently emotionally hurt, she might actually be attracted to men who are emotionally absent, just to get another chance to tame the man who abused her.

People have also been found to be attracted to the ones who share certain similarities with the ones they loved before. If a guy loved a girl but didn't manage to be with her and then meets a girl who looks like her, he might fall for her.

The people we have dealt with in the past can affect the criteria we use when selecting a potential partner. If you had a good friend then for some reason he had to move to another town then there is a good possibility you will feel that you want to become friends with people who look like that person.

If you met someone who looks like your friend, you may become close friends with him. If that friend was from the opposite sex, you might become attracted to him.

The same goes for bad relationships. If you hated a person because of his attitude and then you meet someone who looks like him, you might then feel uncomfortable around that new person, and as a result never become close to him.

Or, if you had a tough boss who used to treat you in a bad way, there is a great possibility you are going to be repelled by whoever reminds you of him consciously or unconsciously.

Emotions and Physical Attraction

Do you know why you get so emotional when watching an important game?

Before I can tell you why this happens let me first tell you about an experiment that was carried out to find out how the brain works.

A monkey was placed in a laboratory and certain wiring connections were made to the area of its brain that was responsible for carrying out movements. Whenever the monkey made a certain move (to grab a peanut for example), the computer registered a sound.

When one of the researches accidentally made a certain move in front of the monkey, the computer made the same sound as well.

In other words, researchers discovered that the same neurons fire when the monkey carries out a task also fire when the monkey sees someone carrying out a task.

These are called "mirror neurons" and they explain why we act as if we are playing a game that we care about while watching it.

Mirror neurons in the human mind are much more complex and advanced than they are in monkeys. They allow us to feel what others are feeling.

When a confident person enters the room, your mirror neurons make you feel good, simply because you absorb some of his confidence. Have you ever watched a scared presenter doing a presentation?

Do you know why you didn't feel comfortable while watching him? It's because your mirror neurons fired and copied his emotions.

Now what does this has to do with attractiveness?

The state of feeling for another person is automatically transferred to others through mirror neurons. That's why confident people and those who have a good sense of humour are found to be much more attractive.

Those who are anxious, afraid, or who lack self confidence transfer these unpleasant emotions to us and that's why we don't enjoy their company.

Studies have found that we associate the emotions we experience in the presence of a person with his personality.

If you go to an exciting movie with someone, you might mistakenly believe that you are excited because of the presence of that person and not because of the movie.

In short, the way you act and feel about yourself affects the emotions of the people you are in the company of, and so impact your overall attractiveness.

Now let's pause for a while and think about it.

Your personality affects the way other perceive your physical attractiveness, yet you don't feel confident around others because you don't like a certain physical feature that you have.

Does this make any sense?

Why men shouldn't be kind to women wearing pink or red

Sounds like a strange title I know, but by the end of this section it wont be anymore. Unlike men, women's preference for attractiveness changes throughout the month. If you ask a man about the things he finds attractive in women then most probably his answer will be the same throughout the month.

Women change their attractivness preferences according to their menstrual cycle. Studies have shown that women become more attracted to masculine men when they are the most fertile and become more attracted to kind men during other parts of the menstrual cycle.

The masculine man isn't the one who has got the muscles but he is the one who perfectly demonstrates male masculinity by:

1) Acting like a leader.
2) Being assertive.
3) Not being a people pleaser.
4) Focusing on his own needs.
5) Not being needy.

During the other stages of the menstrual cycle women become more attracted to men who are kind, sensitive, and caring.

This means that to keep your woman interested in you or to attract someone that you like you need to change your strategy throughout the month.

Now the question is, how can you tell whether this is the time you should be more like a bad boy or a kind man?

The answer is pink!

A study has found that women are three times more likely to wear pink (and red) clothes when they are the most fertile. All women have lots of clothes in their wardrobe, but the reason they pick something to wear on a certain day is that it reflects their psychological state on that day (and usually they are not aware of the reason that motivated them to make the choice).

So a woman wearing pink is more likely to be attracted to a bad boy than a kind, loving guy.

Why do Ugly People Like Me?

A friend of mine once told me that he is worried because lately he has only been attracting ugly people (according to his own opinion about them). My friend had a good point back then.

He said that people pursue the ones they believe they can get and since unattractive people were pursuing him then this might mean that they believe that he is quite attainable.

In other words, his point was, "Had I been good enough they would have never had any hope of getting me, and so they would have never pursued me."

Let me complicate things further by telling you about a study that supports what my friend was saying. A study, which is pretty famous for some unknown reason, says that people pursue the ones who are as attractive as them.

So the study assumes that if I have average looks i will only pursue people who have average looks and so on. So is it really true that being pursued by unattractive people really means that you are unattractive? Let's find out!

Do you remember the last time you pursued someone who was really attractive or a person who is considered much more attractive than you? Do you remember what motivated you to do so?

It's because the person was nice enough to you in such a way that he gave you hope. So we don't actually pursue people who look like us but we go for the ones who give us hope.

Because my friend was kind he treated all people in a good way and because the unattractive ones don't usually get this good treatment they started believing that there might be hope in being with him.

For them my friend was a catch, he is good-looking and at the same time not repelling them the way other attractive than you? No, it only means that she has given you some hope. And because we humans like to become attached to any future possibility that could change our lives we are attracted to those who provide us with hope.

Could it be a pool problem?

In the city my friend lives in a place where beauty is almost non-existent (from his point of view). He knows the good-looking females by name, not because they are stunning, but because there are too few of them. My friend didn't bear this in mind when he was putting forward his argument.

If you are already in a pool that has less desirable people according to your own point of view, then most probably the ones you will attract will not appeal to you.

Finally, as for the study that says that people are attracted to those who look like them, recalling the pictures of the famous celebrities you like will show you in seconds that this study is pure nonsense.

Yes in some cases some people try to be with those who share some common features with themselves due to self love, but this doesn't mean that a totally unattractive person can't fall for an extremely attractive person. And in fact the latter case is the one that happens most often.

So the final conclusion is, attracting unattractive people doesn't mean that you are unattractive by all means, it just means that you were nice to them.

Physical Attractiveness Perception

Physical Attractiveness Perception

Many people feel self-conscious around strangers and become uncomfortable in the company of others because they don't like their own looks.

It's common for a person to feel anxious around strangers due to believing they have an unattractive nose or an unattractive body.

Do you know why do these people feel uncomfortable around others? It's not because they have some physical features that they don't like, it's because they don't know how people perceive physical attractiveness.

Each person sees the world differently and most people focus on the things that concern them the most. A person who doesn't like the shape of his own nose will focus on the other people's noses, especially those who have more attractive ones.

Do you know what this means? It means that only those who are concerned about the shape of their own nose will examine the details of your nose!

By understanding how people perceive physical attractiveness, you will become much more comfortable with your looks, and when this happens your self confidence will skyrocket.

How People See Physical Attractiveness

Earlier in this book I talked about some of the features that people find attractive in others, the point being that many people don't understand how others process these features in their minds when they see you.

Symmetrical faces and women with a low waist to hip ratio are found to be more attractive than others; however, do you know how people perceive this information?

People process your overall looks in search of attractive features and they form their first impression without getting into much detail. This means that your face can appear very attractive to someone even if your nose doesn't look pretty according to your own opinion!

I know a friend who is very attractive according to the opinion of most people who know her. This friend has a tiny scar on her forehead and as a result she becomes self conscious around others because she believes they will judge her by the scar.

She believes that others will focus on the scar, because that's exactly what she does, while the truth is that most people judge her attractiveness as a whole and rarely pay attention to her scar even though they notice it.

Because she is obsessed with her scar, she notices the scars on people's faces in a fraction of a second, then assume that people will do the same to her.

This girl doesn't realize that her perception of physical attractiveness has been modified by her obsession about her facial scar.

Before you start thinking that people will dislike any of your facial features you must remind yourself that everyone sees the world through the lens of his own personal flaws.

The Perception of Attractiveness and your Overall Looks

A few days ago I was walking along a street near my house and a male friend of mine was passing by with his female friend. The guy recognized me from my back and pulled up next to me in his car to say hello. At the same time, I noticed that the girl started sending me attraction signals even though she could barely see me (you will learn more about attraction signals later in this book).

It's clear that she saw me from the back, noticed something as simple as the width of my shoulders and then when she got close she found that my face was almost symmetrical, but not perfect by any means!

This girl found me attractive not because I had perfect facial features, but because the way people perceive physical attractiveness allows them to ignore many of the small details we obsess about.

While at the gym I met a female friend who doesn't think she looks attractive. The first time I saw her I found her very attractive. All I noticed about her during the first encounter was her stylish sports clothes and her fit body. My friend doesn't like her facial features and thinks she is not attractive, while in fact her overall looks gave me the impression that she is very attractive.

In short, people judge your attractiveness based on your overall looks, and it will rarely happen that someone will judge your appearance based on a single facial feature such as your lips or your nose.

This is good news for all those people who dislike any of their facial features , especially women, and think that those features make them ugly.

Why do we Find People Attractive?

Earlier I mentioned that our culture can affect our opinion of attractiveness but the question is, why don't all people within a certain culture find the same person attractive?

Let me ask the question in another way: Why do attraction preferences differ from one person to another within the same culture?

Why would someone find a person attractive, while others find him completely undesirable?

Do you know that your past experiences can make you find certain people attractive?

A girl who was raised by a father who used to ignore her emotional needs will grow up and become an adult who needs excessive care. Such a girl would find any man with facial features that show kindness attractive, provided all the other factors are constant.

The girl won't be aware that she is looking for a person who can give her the care her father failed to provide her with, as all of this will be happening on the subconscious level.

We find people more attractive when we feel that they can help us attain important psychological goals.

That same girl in the previous example will never find a guy attractive if he has a feature or two that are similar to the father's facial features.

Physical attraction is an extremely important factor but what most people don't know is that physical attraction itself can be alerted based upon the person's perceptions. A girl who cares a lot about status will certainly find a man driving a Ferrari more physically attractive than if she saw him going on foot.

Thus, we can find people physically attractive, even if they are average-looking and discover they can help us fulfil our emotional needs.

This means that while there are universal standards for attractiveness imposed on us by globalization, attractiveness is in the eye of the beholder to a great extent.

Attraction between Friends

Why do some people become friends?

Why do some people get along with each other while others don't?

You won't be able to understand how attraction happens perfectly before you know how attraction happens between friends of the same sex well. Note that I am talking about normal straight people who like others and become friends with them as a result.

Also note that many of the rules that apply to friends apply to relationships with the opposite sex as well. This means that many of the things that attract people to each other (to become friends) are the same things that attract members of the opposite sex to each other.

People usually become friends with those who are similar to them. This similarity can happen across any domain starting with physical looks, going through similarities in values and up to similarities in important life goals.

For example:

- ⅄ Two people can become friends just because they have the same opinion about an important political subject.

- ⅄ Two people can become friends because they share similar facial features.

- ⅄ Two people can become friends because they share the same interests.

People tend to look for those who are similar to them because they feel more comfortable around them. People usually make more of an effort to process unfamiliar objects and that's why they feel better around familiar people.

This also explains why the people you spend lots of time with everyday become your friends, i.e. your room mate, or work colleagues. The more time you spend with a person, the more you will feel comfortable around him and the more likely you will become friends with him.

The desire to feel secure whilst being around your friends has a strong influence on the choice of both your friends and your romantic partner

In addition, a recent study has found that people become friends with those who have a high degree of genetic similarity with them. Studies have shown that your friends might be as genetically similar as your fourth cousin.

Complementary Traits and Attraction

People are usually attracted to those who complement them. If it so happens that two people believe they complement each other, they will be attracted to each other.

Sometimes, a person could be attracted to someone just because the latter has something the first doesn't have. Men usually have more confidence than women and are physically stronger, and that's why most women find strong and confident men more attractive.

People can become friends because they complement each other. An ordinary guy might become friends with a rich guy because this allows him to explore the life of rich people. The rich guy, on the other hand, could have become friends with the ordinary guy because he knows how to attract women better than him.

In short, when someone discovers that another person possesses a trait that he doesn't have, then he is usually attracted to him. Between same sex friends, this leads to friendship, while between opposite sexes, this can lead to a romantic relationship.

Social Exchange Theory and Attraction

Social Exchange Theory states that human relationships are governed by the costs the person has to pay to keep the relationship going and the benefits he gets as long as the relationship is still going.

Here is a simple example. If you become friends with someone because he makes you laugh or because he allows you to satisfy an important unmet need you have, such as the need to be loved, and then this person starts becoming annoying and needy, most probably your mind will weigh up both the costs and the benefits to find out which one is higher.

If the benefits are found to be higher, you will still care about the relationship, but if the costs are higher, you might rethink this relationship.

This theory also explains why some couples start disliking each other after some time. Because the chemicals responsible for passion usually fade with time, the other costs of the relationship start to become more visible and people start becoming dissatisfied with the relationship.

Of course people don't stop being friends when the costs of a relationship become higher, but they can sometimes pull back for a while or at least start experiencing dissatisfaction.

Ever tried to avoid one of your friends because he has become so annoying lately?

This is exactly how the costs of a relationship can motivate you to move away from it.

Familiarity and Attractiveness

Studies have shown that people prefer those who are more familiar to them. Each time you see something your brain has to process it. The processing power needed becomes less when something becomes more familiar. People feel more comfortable when they see the faces they are used to see often and that's why familiarity leads to attraction.

People always prefer the things they know over the things they don't know. If you see weird-looking food, then you are very likely to be cautious when tasting it than if you see food you are familiar with.

The more a person is exposed to someone, the more likely he is to become attracted to him. In addition, the ease of processing familiar faces and seeing someone more often might lead to asking the "why not him" question, which is usually the seed that leads to strong attraction.

Once a person starts asking the "why not" question, attraction grows rapidly. The more you are exposed to a person, the more you are likely to ask yourself the "why not be with her" question.

Continued exposure has to be accompanied by pleasant emotions in order for attraction to grow. If, for example, a person has a good sense of humour, then each time people see him they will experience pleasant emotions, and as a result they will be more attached to him.

So, familiarity can lead to attraction when continued exposure to a person results in positive emotions.

Women need more time to become attracted to men than men do. Because men usually rely mostly on visual cues, they can make their mind up about a woman more quickly than a woman about a man.

A person who sees another person more often has a cutting edge advantage over those who see him less often. People who work with others or who go to the same university together have a better chance of attracting those people they meet often than those they don't meet often.

Similarity and Attraction

What is the connection between similarity and attraction theory?
Do likes attract? And, if that's true, how do we sometimes become attracted to those who have complementary personality traits?

For the first question, while those arguments might appear contradictory, in fact, they are perfectly aligned with each other

People are attracted to those they are familiar with. Similarity leads to familiarity. When you meet someone who thinks like you or who shares certain personality traits with you, then you are very likely to find him familiar.

You can also become familiar with someone just because he looks like you or shares certain facial features with you. Some studies have claimed that people are attracted to those who look like them, but in fact people are attracted to those who are similar to them in any way and not just physical looks.

So, similarity is needed for attraction to happen because people prefer the ones they are familiar with over the ones they know nothing about.

In my book, *How to Make Someone Fall in Love with You,* I said that while people become attracted to those who share similar beliefs and certain personality traits with them, they also become attracted to those who posses complementary traits.

Let me give you an example that will make this clear. A shy girl who has a good sense of humour might become attracted to a guy who has a good sense of humour too (similar to her) and who is confident (complementary to her shyness).

So, according to attraction theory, both similarity and complementary traits can be present in the same person, and thus they don't contradict each other by any means.

Remember, when I talked about unmet needs? People are attracted to the ones who are similar to them and who at the same time can help them meet their important unmet needs.

People like those who possess the traits they like about themselves and who at the same time possess the opposite of the traits they don't like about themselves.

Or, a person could dislike you just because you don't look familiar, and not because you look ugly. You could lose the competition against someone who meets your potential target more often, not because you are bad or defective but because the person who sees another person more often usually has an advantage over others.

Similarly in Values

People are attracted more to those who share the same values as them. People only care about the important values and not every value they have. If, for example, a person doesn't care much about a certain value even if he believes in it, then it won't matter if he has found someone who doesn't share that value.

That's why people who care about religion prefer those who share the same religion with them. People who don't give much weight to religion on the other hand, even those who are religious, can still be attracted to a person even if he believes in another religion.

So, it's all about the person's most important values and what he cares about the most. During initial levels of attraction, people can hold on to their opinions; however, if attraction increases past a certain point, some people can actually sacrifice the similarity of values just for the sake of being with that person.

Are People Attracted to Those who Look Like Them?

If you read online about the attraction between opposite sexes then most probably you will come across a web page or a book that tells you that people prefer those who look like them.

Because similarity makes people feel safe. Those writers and researchers assume that people will be attracted to those who look like them, but that's completely incorrect.

Have you met a happy couple where one of them was significantly less physically attractive than the other?

Have you met a gorgeous-looking woman who is married to an average-looking man?

Have you ever liked a person a lot, but your friends tell you that he is not as attractive as you?

The people who came up with this theory didn't quite understand how attraction happens. When people assess the attractiveness of others they do it based on the total score they calculate for the potential partner.

In other words, a person sums up the items that are important to him, gives each of these items a certain weight, then comes up with a total score. This total score is calculated on the unconscious level and it is what determines the attractiveness of a potential partner.

Most people will be attracted to those who possess a similar total score, or even a higher one. A female celebrity will very likely be attracted to another celebrity or a famous businessman simply because their total scores are close to each other's.

Now, if that businessman is not very handsome, his other resources would compensate for his lack of physical beauty , and so his total score will still be high.

Some people claim that the unconscious self-love which is a part of human nature forces people to pick those who look like them. And while this theory makes sense, it won't always be the case that this happens in a similar way in the domain of physical looks. A person who loves himself could pick someone who thinks like him or who has a similar personality.

When you bear in mind that attractiveness happens across many domains, especially for women, you will understand why this theory makes no sense at all.

Do Unattractive People Find Each Other Attractive?

Your self-perceived value can affect your mate's choice. Studies have found that men who don't think they are very desirable find less beautiful women attractive.

It seems that even attractiveness preferences can be changed to help a man find the right partner. If a man believes he is not desirable he might assume he won't be able to get hot women, and as a result his mind lowers his standards of beauty and he finds himself physically attracted to less attractive women.

This effect isn't the same for women as they seem not to sacrifice their needs even when they believe that they can't get what they are after.

The Attractiveness Halo Effect

What is the attractiveness halo effect?

44

It has been found that people assume that good-looking people have additional good traits and qualities.

According to the attractiveness halo effect, it's quite common for people to think that beautiful people are more intelligent, competent, and successful than others.

A lot of research has tested the "attractiveness halo effect," and some of it has found that attractive people receive more help than less attractive ones, while others have found that attractive people get lighter punishments in court if their crime wasn't related to their attractiveness.

According to the "attractiveness halo effect," this phenomenon happens and people aren't consciously aware that the attractiveness of another person has anything to do with their biased judgement.

So, we now know that this attractiveness halo effect is present, but the question is, what causes it?

There are many explanations, but few of them make a lot of sense to me. The continued programming people receive through the media makes them unconsciously associate attractiveness with good qualities.

For example, in any Hollywood movie you will find that the attractive guy is the good guy, the wealthy guy, and the one who always becomes successful at the end of the movie.

I have read an interesting study that said that attractive people are actually more intelligent than non-attractive people. The study claimed that the resourceful man who has above average intelligence and who is successful will usually look for an attractive woman to marry and thus give birth to beautiful and intelligent children!

The attractiveness halo effect can also be explained in the light of the good feelings we get when being around attractive people. When someone makes you feel good, your mind will start to think positively, and as a result you might assign him good qualities even if you know nothing about him.

Provided that all the other factors are equal, attractive people are more likely to get better jobs, have more friends, and earn more money!

Could this all be happening because of the attractiveness halo effect?
Yes this might be possible because, after all, success in life is heavily dependent upon your relationships with others and if most people believe that you have many good qualities then you will certainly get more opportunities than others.

Physical Proximity and Attraction

Most studies have found that people get into a relationship with those who live nearby. In the previous section I said that the more a person is exposed to another person, the more he tends to like her.

In psychology, this is called the mere exposure effect. This is the increased likeability of something as a result of being exposed to it more often.

Since physical proximity assists in making people more familiar, it has been found that physical closeness can lead to emotional closeness.

This is also why we might forget about a person when he travels or moves away. The good news is that in the age of Internet this physical proximity can be compensated for to a certain extent by online presence.

The more you are exposed to a person online the more you are likely to like him, provided that all the other variables are constant. This is why it's always a good idea to stick around the person you like because your chance of attracting him will increase.

How our Emotions Affect our Perception of Attraction

Studies have found that our emotions tend to affect our perception of attractiveness. This means that you might incorrectly associate your pleasant emotions with the presence of a particular person.

For example, if you are enjoying a movie in the presence of a friend then you might actually believe you had fun because of the presence of the friend and not because of the movie.

The famous experiment known as the "Bridge of Love" can better illustrate this concept. The volunteers in the experiment were divided so that half of them had to walk on a safe suspension bridge while the others had to walk on a scary one that seemed unstable.

During their walk on the bridge they were stopped by a female researcher who asked them some questions and told them she would wait for their feedback.

The number of people who called back on the scary bridge was much higher than the number of those who called back on the safe bridge.

This happened because the excitement that resulted from walking on an unsafe bridge was unconsciously associated with the female researcher. In other words, the people thought that they were excited because of the presence of the female researcher!

Another study has found that people tend to find others less attractive when the temperature of the room is too hot or too cold. This means that any external factor that makes a personal uncomfortable can affect his perception of physical attractiveness!

In other words, people could rate you less attractive than you really are just because they are not in a good mood.

It has also been found that people tend to be more critical of the looks of the people they don't like.

If someone is jealous of you, then most likely he is going to focus on your flaws, and as a result, he will find you less attractive. Some people actually make harsh remarks to others about their attractiveness.

Because most people don't think they look exactly movie heroes, they take those comments personally without thinking for a second that jealousy could be the main reason behind it.

By the way, jealousy happens across sexes, a person can became jealous of your success even if he is from the opposite sex, and as a result the bad comment you got about your looks might be caused by jealousy even if it came from the opposite sex.

Finding One Flaw Leads to Finding the Rest

In one study, experimenters persuaded subjects to treat different subjects in three different ways.

Some subjects were treated in a cruel way, others were treated In a generous way and a third group was treated in a neutral way.

It was found that people started to dislike the ones they treated in a cruel way and to like the ones they treated in a generous way.

In other words, human beings tend to try and justify their actions even if they are forced to do them just like in the experiment.

Again, this shows that a person could find you unattractive just because he is jealous of you.

A Quick Summary - Why Each Person Judges Attractiveness Differently

Many people dislike their looks because the way they judge attractiveness differs from the way others judge their attractiveness. Once these people get to know the fact that most people judge attractiveness differently, they come to realize that they are considered attractive according to the other people's opinions.

Even though the media has promoted certain standards of attractiveness and programmed the people's minds along with them, there are many factors that make people judge physical attractiveness differently. Here are some of them:

- **Past experience:** If you have a horrible boss who doesn't treat you well then most likely you are going to hate him. Now, if you see someone who looks like that boss you will believe that he is much less attractive than he really is. The subconscious mind of a person responds to subtle clues that the conscious mind hardly notices. You don't have to see a person who looks like your boss to believe he has got the same personality, you just need to see someone who has one or two prominent facial features that resemble your boss's face! In other words, if a person has the same nose and chin as your boss, then you might find him unattractive without even noticing how your subconscious mind came to such a conclusion.

- **The relationship with parents:** Our relationship with our parents alters our perception of attractiveness to a great extent. If a girl loves her father a great deal then most probably she will find any man who has facial features that resemble her father very attractive. The opposite will happen if that girl hates her father, in such a case, she will find men who look like him much less attractive.

- **Priorities differ from one person to another:** One man might be obsessed with a woman who has proportional features; another man might become obsessed with a

47

woman who has a fit body, while a third man might become obsessed with classy women. Even though the world agrees on certain standards of beauty, the priority of these standards differs from one person to another.

⚊ **Compensation and physical attractiveness perception:** Physical attractiveness perception changes according to how you look and how you believe you look. A dark man might be attracted to white women if he believes that he would look better if he was white. This kind of compensation alters the attractiveness perception of a person.

The conclusion you should come up with is that even if you believe you are not an attractive person, other people might find you attractive! If you dislike the shape of your nose, then this doesn't mean that everyone will have the same opinion about it, simply because people see the world differently.

The love map

Each person has his own love map which determines the kind of people who he will find attractive. Even identical twins could have different love maps and so never fall in love with the same person.

However, just as each person has his own love map that differs from others people are also bound by certain biological factors that determine the kind of people they are attracted to.

For example, any man in the world would be attracted to women who have a low waist to hip ratio (around 0.8), unless he has been through devastating life experiences that have forced him to override his biological preferences.

The same goes for women, while each woman might have a different love map, there are still some common factors that would be on the list of almost every normal woman.

Do Women Like Guys Who Ride Motorbikes?

All women have a need for protection. This is why the strong, confident, macho, and brave man attracts most women.

Based on this need for protection, women assign a high weight to certain traits such as courage. After all, if a man is brave then he will be better able to protect her and her child. Now, when a woman sees a man riding a motorbike she automatically assumes that he is brave. After all, if you try to talk about motorbikes anywhere the first thing you hear from people is that they are dangerous.

In the past men were supposed to be warriors and women were supposed to be gatherers of food. No matter how technology advances it seems that the old brain is still in control of so many of our desires. Long ago a woman used to find a man riding a horse more attractive than those who don't ride because riding signified courage.

Now the reptilian part of a woman's brain can't really tell the difference between a man riding a horse and a man riding a motorbike, and as a result both are found equally attractive.

In addition to the fact that women are attracted to brave men, many of them like adventurous ones, and this is another conclusion that is usually made when a man is seen on a motorbike.

That's Me on a Motorbike

Do I have to ride a bike in order to be considered attractive?

The short answer is No!

In the previous pages I said that even though most women are biologically wired to prefer taller men, short men still have a good chance if they manage to show the woman that they can protect her.

In other words, women like tall men because they unconsciously think they are more capable of protecting them. Now if the short man shows that he can do the same thing then the woman might overlook the height issue.

The great thing about attraction psychology is that you can send the same message across different domains. For example, a woman can still find you brave and adventurous even if you don't ride a motorbike, provided that you display courage across any other domain.

Do men with dogs have a better chance?

Do men with dogs have better chance of attracting women?
The short answer is Yes!

Studies have shown that men who own dogs have a higher chance of attracting women. One study has shown that a man will have a much higher chance of talking to a woman if he has bought a dog.

Women rarely take the first step, but when you have a dog things can turn the other way around and you might find a woman approaching you just to play with your dog.

So what is it exactly that makes men with dogs more attractive to women?

Why Women Like Men with Dogs

Women are more selective when it comes to choosing a life partner. While men might focus on few traits when making a choice, women take more time to asses whether that man can make a good parent or not.

In other words, when selecting a potential mate women take into consideration a man's ability to raise healthy children.

Here is why women like men with dogs:

- **1) Commitment type:** Women always look for subtle signals that reflect the personality traits they are looking for. When they see a man with a dog they usually assume that he is the kind of a man who can commit to a long-term relationship. Because raising a dog and taking care of it requires a lot of commitment and dedication many women make that conclusion about men who own dogs.

- **2) Lack of selfishness:** It's extremely hard for a selfish person to raise a pet. After all, if a man is willing to give some of his time and money to a pet then won't he do that when he has kids? This is exactly how women think when they see a man with a dog. They tend to assume that this kind of man can raise better children because he is generous and not selfish.

- **3) Kindness:** Most women want men who treat them well, and nothing can give a better indication of kindness than the way a man treats his pet. Men with dogs are usually perceived to be kinder and friendlier than other men. A typical woman believes that a man who is kind to his dog will usually be kind to his family.

- **4) Good chance to approach men:** Many women want to take the first step but are pressured by society's norms. Now when these women approach a man who has a dog they feel at ease because they assume that this man will believe that they just want to play with his dog and nothing more.

- **5) Extroversion and social skills:** Dog owners are usually extroverts who have good social skills. Because many women like a man who can handle people well they tend to find men with dogs more attractive than other men provided that all the other factors are constant.

It's all about finding the right father

just as you have seen, women want a man who can take care of their family and protect it. Because many of these traits can be visible through the way men treat their dogs, women tend to be attracted to men who have dogs.

Men who have cats might seem a bit suspicious to women. After all, a typical man usually prefers to look after a dog than a cat and that's why some women might question the reasons that made a man look after a cat.

The available options v. the options you are aware of

An available option is the one you believe you can get if you make some effort, but this doesn't mean that there aren't any better options out there that are out of your reach.

The options you are exposed to, on the other hand, are all the potential targets you have encountered throughout your life, including the ones you believe you couldn't get.

A person who has seen a lot is always hard to please simply because his mind always compares the new people he meets to the database of the people he has met throughout his life. But there is another factor that determines how the perception of attractiveness changes, which is a person's self-esteem.

If the person believes that he can attract those beautiful new people he's encountered, then most probably he will raise his attractiveness standards. On the other hand, if that person has low self esteem then being exposed to more beautiful people might only motivate him to back off and to stick to the less attractive ones.

How your Experience Database Affects your Perception of Attractiveness

If a man lives in a country that has low standards of beauty, then most probably the database of people this person has been exposed to won't include extremely beautiful ones, and as a result he might find a woman with average attractiveness very attractive!

On the other hand if this man travels to a new country that has more beautiful women and spends some time there, then most probably his perception of attractiveness will change and he won't find the women of his own country as attractive as before.

This is also why psychologists believe that the media is committing a great crime against society with its movies and TV commercials. The more people are exposed to such movies and commercials the more their standards of beauty shoot up and the less they are satisfied with average-looking people.

This change in perception can also be situational. If you go to a new school where most people are not that attractive then a person with an average level of attractiveness will become very appealing to you just because he is the most attractive person there, and not because he really is attractive.

If a girl goes to a yoga class and encounters nine females and one average-looking male, then most probably this male will become much more desirable than if he were seen in class that had other attractive males.

Why people judge physical attractiveness differently

Each and every person has a different database of the people he has encountered during his life. As a result people judge the physical attractiveness of others differently.

If a person works as an actor and is constantly exposed to very attractive people then most likely he will find most average-looking people much less desirable.

So your experience database affects your perception of attractiveness to a great extent. One good point is that even if you are not that attractive this doesn't necessarily mean that people will find you unattractive because it all depends on their own knowledge database and the people they have been exposed to during their lives!

Things That Have Nothing To Do With Your Looks

Attractiveness is not Just About Looks

Almost all people make that same mistake when they think about their overall attractiveness, which is focusing on one element, such as facial attractiveness, while ignoring all the other factors involved.

While men are attracted to women who have proportional facial features and full lips, they can still be attracted to a woman even if they haven't seen her face. If a man sees a woman from a distance and she appears to be fit, then he will consider her attractive even though he hasn't seen her face.

That same woman might think that men will find her unattractive just because her nose doesn't look perfect.

When people judge the attractiveness of others they take into consideration the full package and not just facial features. People don't consider someone attractive when all of his features are attractive. Instead, one attractive feature such as being fit can alter the overall attractiveness of a person to a great extent.

The same goes for a woman who might find a man attractive just because she notices that he is well-dressed. Again, the attractiveness of the man's clothes boosts his overall attractiveness and makes women consider him attractive.

Here are few items that can alter the overall attractiveness of a person:

- Wearing elegant clothes.

- Overall cleanliness.

- Wearing accessories that reflect a high social status.

- Balanced body shape.

Just as you may now have come to realise, your attractiveness levels can be manipulated to a great extent. Even if you don't like one of your facial features you can still appear attractive to others!

I Want So and So

People are attracted to others on an unconscious level. This is why the wish list of most people, especially women, has nothing to do with the person they end up with.

Ask any person about the things he wishes to find in his potential partner, then wait until he gets into a relationship. Most probably you will discover that the person he ended up with has nothing to do with the person he wished for.

Women usually fantasize about popular celebrities then end up with people who share nothing with them!

Men usually know what they are looking for more than women, or in other words men use their conscious mind a bit more when they are seeking a potential partner.

Because men's minds are much simpler when it comes to attraction psychology, many men can end up with people who resemble their wish list.

When both men and women find a person who matches their unconscious criteria, they are quickly attracted to him forgetting about many of the items they previously had on their wish list.

Understanding human behaviour

for any unusual human behaviour there is usually an explanation, which you get from the person who is involved and the real motive behind it.

In order to understand human behaviour you need to forget about the words people say and focus on understanding the way their brains work. After all a showy person isn't going to tell you that he married a blond in order to show off, but he will tell you that he fell in love with her (and he won't be lying).

Ask any man who prefers older women why he is attracted to them and most probably he will give you a reason that has nothing to do with his real motives simply because he doesn't understand his own motives.

The second thing you need to know about human behaviour is that more than one person can engage in the same behaviour for different reasons. This means that two men could be attracted to older women for two completely different reasons.

Why do Some Men Prefer Older Women?

Bear in mind that I am not talking about special cases where a man loves a woman then discovers that she is older than him, but I am talking about men who are mostly attracted to women after they discover that they are older than them.

So why do some men prefer older women? Here are some possible explanations:

- **1) In need of a mother figure:** Human beings use love to satisfy their most important unmet needs. If a man didn't get enough nurturing from his mother, or if his mother was absent in one way or another, then he might start being attracted to older women. Because the subconscious mind believes that an older woman can provide that man with the love he was deprived of it will make him attracted to older women

- **2) Childhood and past experiences:** Spoiled children, only children, and the ones who were showered with excessive care might develop the need to be taken care of, and this need might remain even when they become adults. In such a case those men might be attracted to older women because they want someone to take care of them the same way they used to be.

- **3) Raising their self esteem:** Older women usually have fewer choices and as a result they become more devoted to their men. This kind of devotion raises the self esteem of that man since the woman he is with idolizes him and showers him with attention.

- **4) To feel superior:** Some men seek older women in order to feel superior. After all, managing to attract someone from a parallel world can provide a strong Ego boost to most people. I once met a guy in his late twenties, and he was showing off about his ability to attract women in their forties. This made him feel special or superior to his peers. This feeling becomes stronger if this woman has a high status, and because many older woman have good careers their status is usually higher than the status of younger women.

- **5) Sexual Fantasies:** Men are turned on by sexual novelty and they might get bored if they remain with the same partner throughout their life unless that partner knows how to always keep the man interested. Men will always go after new experiences if they have the chance. Being with an older woman is one of the sexual phases that many men might pass through and as a result they might find themselves attracted only to them.

Sexual desire and attraction to older women

There is one very important fact you should understand about sexual desire. The brain uses sexual desire to help humans satisfy their psychological needs. In other words, if a man tells you that he is attracted to an older woman because of sexual desire then know that there is another underlying reason apart from sexual attraction.

The man who says so won't be lying because he simply might not be aware of the fact that sexual desire can be a tool his subconscious mind uses to help him reach a bigger goal.

People who don't understand how others perceive physical attraction usually develop the imagined ugliness disorder.

Women and Bad Boys

A study was carried out to find out the kind of faces that attract women. Women were shown pictures of men, then these pictures were modified using a computer to make them look more masculine.

The study found that women prefer masculine faces, and this already agreed with what biology says, but when the results were examined further it was found that women were attracted to men who seemed more threatening!

Women were found to be attracted to men who seemed more dangerous, and this supports the findings other studies have come up with, which is that women tend to be attracted to bad boys.

Women are attracted to men who take charge, who are dominant and assertive. Bad or dangerous-looking guys appear to have these traits, and that's why women find them attractive.

Women are also attracted to men who seem to be more dangerous than others because of the excitement they feel around them. Women dislike boring men who have a traditional personality and instead prefer the risk-taker who can bring them a lot of excitement.

Ask any woman about the type of guy she wants to be with and she will respond saying that she wants a nice guy who treats her well. Now wait until she gets into a relationship and you will discover that she is attached to the bad boy who abuses her.

A typical bad boy is the one who runs the relationship according to his own rules; he is cocky and arrogant, and he does what he wants with no regard to what others think.

Nice guys, who are the opposite of bad boys, turn most women off. Nice guys are needy, they don't take the lead, and are highly predictable.

The reason women like bad boys is that this combination of narcissism, thrill-seeking behaviour, and dominance are seen as signs of masculinity, which is one of the ultimate attraction factors for women.

One explanation in relation to the mystery of women's attraction to bad boys who abuse them is the challenge of attaining the unattainable.

Bad boys are hard to get, they are mysterious, and not by any means needy. As a result of this combination of traits, these bad boys seem like a challenge to most women.

We all know that the more unattainable something is, the more attractive we find it to be. Many women go for bad boys just because they want to go through the challenge of taming the person who can't be tamed.

The self-esteem boost women get when they tame a bad boy can be great and that's why they go for him even though they know that he might be an abusive partner.

One thing that attracts women the most is self confidence. Just as men are turned on by a woman's looks, women are turned on by a man's confidence.

Bad boys are usually rule breakers, risk takers, and adventurers. Women process these traits as a sign of confidence, and that's one reason why they are attracted to bad boys.

Nice guys, on the other hand, appear to be weak to most women. Women usually interpret the actions of a nice guy as signs of weakness, and since women are biologically wired to look for strong and protective men, they are turned off by nice guys.

Women Change their Preferences for Physical Attractiveness

Women change their preference for physical attractiveness throughout their menstrual cycle, thus adding to the complexity of the process of mate selection they use!

During the time when women are most fertile, when they are ovulating, they are attracted to men who have more masculine features and who are more like bad boys.

During other parts of the menstrual cycle, women tend to be attracted to males who have more feminine features!

This means that what a certain woman finds attractive during a certain day of the month, is subject to major changes during other days of the same month!

From a biological point of view, this can be explained as follows:

Women are attracted to masculine men when they are most fertile because mating with such a man will increase the likelihood of pregnancy, in addition to bearing healthy offspring.

On the other hand, women need a caring and loving man to take care of their offspring during other parts of the cycle, when she is not as fertile.

The need to have healthy and strong offspring fuels a woman's desire to be with a muscular man during ovulation, and her desire for intimacy during other stages of the cycle fuels her desire to be with a kind man.

This means that the day on which you meet a woman can determine to what extent she will find you attractive based on the stage she is going through in her menstrual cycle.

As I said earlier, women respond to different cues across many domains when assessing a man's attractiveness. That's why even if you don't have the facial features a woman is looking for during a certain stage of her menstrual cycle, you can still send her the same message using a different channel.

For example, if you don't have the tough masculine look you can still make a woman think you are more masculine than others by acting in a more masculine way.

During the time when a woman is ovulating, she will be more attracted to the bad boy type. Being assertive, confident, less needy, and more in control will make your woman more attracted to you during that time.

During other stages of the cycle, you should work on being more of a good listener, more caring, and friendlier than you were during the time the woman was ovulating.

If you manage to change the way you deal with your woman during the different stages of her menstrual cycle, then she will become much more attached to you.

People fall in love with those who can satisfy their important unmet needs, just as a woman's needs change throughout the month because of the effect hormones have on their brains.

The unmet needs people have are not constant and they change as they keep growing and learning. An overwhelming experience that a person goes through might change his unmet needs, and in turn, his preferences for physical attraction.

The key to making a person become attached to you is understanding his unmet needs perfectly and working on helping him satisfy them.

It has also been found that women become more attracted to masculine facial features and personality traits when they are looking for a short-term partner. When women look for a short-term partner they tend to care more about genetic quality and dominance. However, when a woman is looking for a long-term partner, she may prefer males with more feminine faces.

For example, a study was carried out where women were asked to pick one man for a long-term relationship and one man for a short-term one. The study found that women preferred caregivers (who had more feminine faces) over dominant males (who had more masculine faces) when they were picking a long-term partner.

The opposite happened when women were asked to pick a short-term partner.

How Hormonal Changes Affect Females Preferences for Men

Women respond to different cues across many domains when assessing a man's attractiveness. That's why even if you don't have the facial features a woman is looking for during a certain stage of her menstrual cycle you can still send her the same message using a different channel.

For example, if you don't have the tough masculine look you can still make a woman think that you are more masculine than others by acting in a more masculine way.

During the time when a woman is ovulating she will be more attracted to the bad boy type. Being assertive, confident, less needy, and more in control will make your woman be more attracted to you during that time.

During other stages of the cycle you should work on being more of a good listener, more caring, and friendlier than you were during the time the woman was ovulating.

If you manage to change the way you deal with your woman during the different stages of her menstrual cycle then she will become much more attached to you.

The Effects of Smell

Many studies have explored the effects of the smell of a human being on the attraction process. In one study some men were allowed to sweat, then women were given the shirts belonging to those men and were asked to tell who the most attractive man was just from the smell.

It was found that women were attracted the most to the man who had the most different immune system. When God designed human beings he wanted healthier generations to be born all the time, and as a result he designed human beings in such a way that they are attracted to those who have a different immune system.

When two people with different immune systems bring a child into the world, it is more likely that the child will have immunity against a larger number of diseases than each of his parents.

Another experiment was carried out to determine how a man's smell affects his attractiveness ratings. Women were asked to rate the attractiveness of several men shown in pictures.

While those women were rating the pictures they were exposed to pleasant and unpleasant smells, and the results were:

⋏	Women rated men's faces as significantly less attractive in the presence of unpleasant smells! They also found men much more attractive when they were exposed to pleasant smells!

⋏	The research clearly states that you will appear more attractive to women if you smell good than if you look good!

⋏	Smell affects the overall mood of a person and can even motivate him to take certain actions. It was also found that some smells motivate people to buy more goods, and that's why they are used some stores.

⋏	Another study suggests that a pleasant smell can affect mood more than looks, music, sounds and touch!

⋏	If a certain smell makes a person experience pleasant feelings, there is a great chance that others will associate happy feelings with the presence of that person. In other words, the use of a good perfume can affect your desirability in an indirect way.

⋏	Another researcher found that when women are ovulating they produce certain pheromones that increases the testosterone levels of a man who smells them!

Again, it can be said that God designed men and women this way because he wanted mating to happen when women are most fertile.

Women Change their Preference for the Way Men Smell

Studies have found that women find the way men smell more appealing when they are ovulating. When women are at the most fertile stage of their cycle, they prefer the smell of men who have symmetrical faces.

Here is how one study that proved this fact was carried out:

Some men were allowed to wear T-shirts for two days, then after that the T-shirts were sent to women to smell them and rate the attractiveness of their smell.

The women were divided into three groups. The first consisted of women who were around the time of ovulation; the second of women who were at other parts of the cycle where conception was less unlikely, and the third was a group of women who were on contraceptive pills.

The women in the first group, where conception was most likely, found the smell of the T-shirts of those men who had symmetrical faces more attractive than the women who were at other stages of the cycle.

Women who were on contraceptive pills seemed to be unaffected by men's smell! In other words, women become more sensitive to the way men smell when they are ovulating and from a biological point of view this makes a lot of sense because:

Facial symmetry is a good indication of health and the presence of good genes which can be passed on to a child, and when women are most fertile they are attracted to the smell of those men who have symmetrical faces and this results in healthier offspring.

When Time is About to Run Out

Another study has found that people find members of the opposite sex more attractive when they are about to leave a public place. The fear of going home alone or staying single for another day makes people find others more attractive.

So, what does this has to do with attracting someone?

Ageing is one of the most powerful factors in affecting choice of mate. The more a person ages, the more he feels that he might end up single and the more likely his perception of beauty is to change.

This happens more often with women than men, since women have a limited number of years where they are fertile. A woman who once had very high standards could lower them a great deal if she feels that she is getting older.

This brings us to another important related topic concerning the available options.

If a woman believes she is very attractive, then she will believe she has more options, and as a result she will become more "picky."

In other words, some people are picky because they believe that they have a large pool to choose from even if no ideal options are available right now.

That's another reason why people who are too confident might stay single for a long time. While they are meeting good people, they still believe they can do better.

If a woman has few options, let's say because her lifestyle doesn't allow her to meet many new people, then most likely she will sacrifice some of her needs when choosing a life partner. If that woman wants a man who has seven good specific personality traits, then she might sacrifice two of them just because she believes she won't be able to find a better man.

This way of thinking might lead to cheating later on! When a person makes a choice just because he has no more options, then one day, when he finds a better option, he might become a cheater.

When choosing a life partner, don't consider the available options, try to find out what you really want while disregarding what's available.

Back to that beautiful girl who believes she can get any man she wants. If her life changes in a way that makes her believe that she now has less options, she might sacrifice some of her demands as well.

Ageing is one example of a change that can make a woman feel that she has fewer options. If that woman is obsessed about staying young, there is a good possibility she will sacrifice some of her needs when she gets older.

Here in the Middle East, where the average marriage age is around 25, it's so common for a woman to be less demanding after the age of 25, just because she is afraid of ending up alone.

So, here again the parameters governing the available options greatly affect a woman's choice.

People never fall in love except with those who meet their subconscious criteria (the list of traits and resources that a person might have in order to be attractive according to their own point of view).

Now, when bearing in mind the available options a person has, you will be able to figure out to what extent he is willing to sacrifice some of his needs.

In other words, if a person has few options then you don't have to meet all of his subconscious criteria in order to make him fall in love with you. You just need to meet the basic ones.

Finding Someone Less Attractive Later On

I am sure you used to like someone long ago then found him less attractive over time. This might have happened because many new options showed up and as a result you realized that you have different needs than the ones you thought you had.

Whether you are trying to attract a person or whether you are trying to understand how your mind works, examining the parameters governing the available options will give you a better understanding of yourself and others.

Why you should never go shopping with someone you don't want to date

This sounds like a weird title right? What's the problem with going shopping with someone you know? Is it that you'll become attached to that person if you go shopping with him often?

No. But a person who goes shopping with you will collect vital information about how your mind works and he can easily use it against you to make you fall in love with him.

Confused yet? Then continue reading.

I also said that once you understand how this love map works you can easily show someone that you are the kind of person who matches all the criteria on his love map and so make him fall in love with you. For a detailed explanation about this process check out my latest video:

So what does love has to do with shopping?

Here is the surprising news: it has been found that the mechanism of selecting a potential partner is very similar to the mechanism of choosing an item to buy while shopping.

Here are a few examples that will make things clear:

- **1) Example one:** Sarah and James went shopping. Sarah liked how a pair of shoes looked, but when she tried them she didn't feel comfortable and so she didn't buy them. This means that in order for Sarah to fall in love with you she must be comfortable around you even if you aren't the best-looking guy around.

- **2) Example two:** Ryan was torn between two watches, but when both of his friends insisted that the grey one was better he bought it. In other words, in order to attract Ryan you need to impress his friends first because he usually believes them even if he initially had another opinion.

- **3) Example three:** Jason tried a pair of shoes that he liked but he didn't buy them. Instead he went home and came back three days later after making up his mind. In such a case you can safely assume that Jason is not the kind of person who will feel comfortable if he gets close to someone fast. This is why the best way to approach him is slowly and gradually.

Depending on the shopping process alone to collect information about someone's love map isn't a good idea, simply because each and every thing a person does reveals more information about the kind of potential partner he is looking for.

How psychological factors affect sexual desire

Most people work in order to make a living, but why would a billionaire keep working even though he has all the money he needs?

It's because his work is allowing him to fulfill another important psychological goal. This goal could be satisfying his Ego, protecting his identity, or maintaining his status.

In other words, human beings can be doing the same things for completely different reasons. We all know that people have sex in order to satisfy their sexual desires, but what most people aren't aware of is that sometimes people have sex to achieve a completely different goal.

Lots of things take place in the subconscious mind of a person that aren't usually noticed by his conscious mind. Sometimes a person's subconscious mind motivates him to do a certain action without giving him any explanation.

This is why some people have psychological disorders; it's because their subconscious minds are trying to reach certain goals that they aren't consciously aware of.

So what does all this has to do with sex?

How Psychological Factors Affect Sexual Desire

Some people feel unloved. These people usually follow any path that enables them to get some of the love they need. Without realizing the reason these people can become sex addicts who try to have sex with anyone they encounter.

While all normal humans should crave sex to fulfill their desires sex, addicts crave sex in order to fulfill a completely different goal, which in this case is feeling loved.

Some other people use sex to raise their self esteem. "Players" are a perfect example of people who seek many sexual partners in order to raise their self-esteem, which is usually low.

A typical player will feel more confident with each victim he catches, and because he is always in need of approval he can hardly give up his habit unless he understands what's going on.

A third group of people seek sex in order to feel in control over others. Men who don't feel that dominant when it comes to dealing with women might seek sex in order to feel that they are dominant and in control.

Differences in sexual desire between men and women

A man's sexual desire only requires the presence of the right visual clues in order to be activated, while a woman's sexual desire requires the presence of more complex psychological factors.

While a man can be turned on through sight, a woman must quickly process many things in her brain before she can decide whether she will be turned on or not. That's why women who get married to people they don't really love report low sexual desire.

In other words, women need to be psychologically turned on as much as men need to be biologically turned on. That's why drug companies have failed to create a drug similar to Viagra for women. While they have managed to control the biological factors involved in the arousal of women, they have failed to control the psychological factors involved. The final conclusion is that humans can be involved in certain behavior in order to fulfill certain unconscious goals that they are unaware of.

People who don't understand how others perceive physical attraction usually develop a imagined ugliness disorder.

Why do Some Men Lose Interest in Women after Having Sex?

Why do some men lose interest in certain women after having sex?
I get many messages from women who say that they are unhappy because their men left them for good a few days or weeks after having sex.

This problem begins with a lack of understanding of the way men think. A woman will chase a man if she likes him (in most cases), but a man can chases a woman for different reasons. A man might be chasing you because he likes you or just because he wants to have sex.

I get many messages from a lot of confused women who tell me that some men send them messages and say that they love them, and then do the opposite; I usually reply saying that many men will do whatever it takes just to reach the goal of having sex.

In other words, many women are too naive to realize that some men can lie, act as if they have emotions, and make up a lot of stories just to end up having sex.

While most women usually have the goal of bonding with a partner that they love, many men are seeking sex and nothing else.

At this point you may have guessed that men who lose interest after having sex are the ones who wanted nothing but sex, and that's correct. But the question is, why do those men lose interest and start chasing other women?

If, for example, a man fails to get into a relationship with a certain woman then he will get turned on by any other woman who shares a few similar features with her, even if the similarity couldn't be noticed on a conscious level.

A man might be attracted to a woman who has the same eyes or nose of his favorite actress without noticing the similarities with his conscious mind.

In other words, past unfinished business can control a man's sexual desire and determine the type of woman he is attracted to.

In other cases some men are physically attracted to certain women just because they want to control them, feel superior to them, or because of any other psychological reason.

What can a woman do about that?

Here in the Middle East most couples never have sex before marriage, and these traditions solve a very big part of the problem. If the man isn't of the commitment type and if he only wants sex then he will give up and lose hope whenever he finds that he has to commit, or that the cost he will have to pay to have sex is too much.

In other cultures where couples can be in a relationship even if they are not married I advise women to avoid sex during the early phases in order to test the man. A man who has no goal in mind but to have sex will always be impatient and won't be able to wait for a long time.

If he isn't allowed to reach his goal in the first few weeks then he will certainly leave and pursue another woman. By doing this you will be able to filter out those who are not serious about the relationship.

The Kind of Man Women Like

So many articles describe a bad boy as a guy who has tattoos, a leather jacket, and a motorbike, while in fact things are much more complex than this superficial description.

Ever seen a guy and felt threatened?
Ever seen a guy and thought that this is the kind of guy you don't want to pick a fight with?

Well, this is typically the kind of man who attracts most women. He looks threatening, intimidating, and strong. He will definitely be extremely assertive, he will be very sure of himself, he won't be smiling at everyone, and his external appearance will give the impression that he slightly aggressive.

I am sure that many women have told you that they want to be with a sensitive and caring guy, but when it comes to understanding people you should not give any weight to what they say, but rather to what they do.

Most women fall for the bad boy and consider bringing out his sensitive side to be a challenge. Now, because that man has become more of a challenge women get more excited about him.

Compare this to the guy who bought flowers and was extremely nice from day one. Is there any kind of an interesting challenge here?

This is why a nice guy always loses

While the previous traits might make a person less friendly, they still send many indirect messages that women get. Here they are:

- **1) This man can protect me:** The bad boy seems strong enough to women, and as a result they assume that he is a good source of protection.

- **2) He doesn't need me:** Being needy pushes anyone away, and because the bad boy is anything but needy, women find him more attractive.

- **3) He is confident:** Confidence is one of the traits that attract women the most. Now because the bad boy is assertive and not desperate for love or attention he appears much more confident than other guys.

The Face

What Makes a Face Pretty?

There are many things that collectively determine the overall attractiveness of a human face.

The first of these elements is facial symmetry. Facial symmetry means that the right side of the face should be almost identical to the left side of the face.

However, no human being has two identical facial parts, but the closer those parts to each other, the more attractive the person is perceived to be .

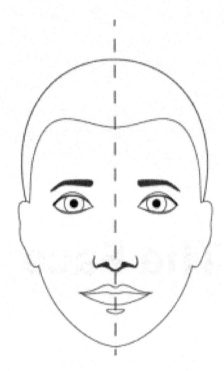

Facial symmetry is associated with health. It has been found that people with more symmetrical faces have better genes and better overall health.

That's why humans were designed to go for those who have symmetrical faces. When a person is attracted to another healthy person, the resulting offspring will be healthier.

Many people obsess about the shape of a certain feature in their face while forgetting to look at other important things such as facial symmetry.

One study found that babies tend to stare more at attractive faces. When more investigations were made, it was found that babies tend to look more at symmetrical faces.

It is also worth mentioning that perfect symmetry can have a negative impact on your looks. When saying that symmetrical faces are attractive, I actually mean faces that are almost symmetrical.

When computer images were generated of perfectly symmetrical faces they were found to look artificial and unattractive.

Attractiveness and Health

It has been found that the more attractive a person is, the fewer health problems he suffers from. The diseases people get while they are growing affect their genes and result in an overall change to their looks.

Some studies say that people with longer faces tend to get respiratory problems, while those with shorter faces tend to get lots of headaches.

The more symmetrical a person's face is, the fewer health problems he suffers from and the better his genes are. When you like someone who looks very pretty you are actually attracted to the healthiest person according to your subconscious mind's point of view.

Human beings were designed that way in order to bring the healthiest offspring into the world.

Facial Proportions

The golden ratio is a ratio that is found everywhere in nature. The golden ration is found in the proportions of flowers, trees, animals, and human beings.

The golden ratio is 1 to 1.6, and its presence in the human face boosts the overall attractiveness of the face.

Ideally, facial width to facial height should abide by the golden ratio. In other words, the ratio of a face's width to its height should be 1 to 1.6.

- The eyes should be half way between the top of the head and the chin.

- The bottom of the nose should be half way between the eyes and the chin.

- The mouth should be one third of the distance between the nose and the chin.

- The distance between the eyes should be equal to the width of one eye.

- The corner of the mouth must line up with the centre of the eyes.

- The top of the ears must line up slightly above the eyes.

- The bottom of the ears should line up with the bottom of the nose.

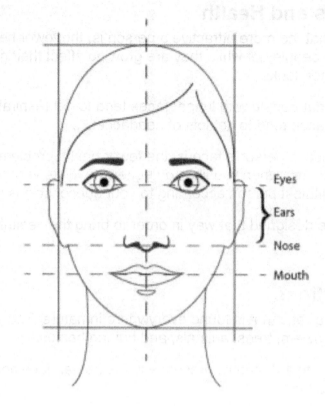

Individual features increase the attractiveness of a face when their sizes are proportional to the size of the face. A big nose, very small eyes, or any feature that is not proportional can reduce the overall attractiveness of a face.

In other words facial proportions is one of the biggest factors that determines the overall attractiveness of a person.

The Feminine v. the Masculine Look

For women, any feature that enhances their overall femininity and gives a more feminine look is considered attractive. Large eyes, full lips, a small chin, high cheek bones, and a small nose make a woman look more feminine and more attractive.

The same goes for men; any facial feature that asserts a man's masculinity will be considered attractive. A big jaw, thick eyebrows, and prominent cheek bones are all features that make a man look more masculine and more attractive.

Facial Scars

Studies have found that women find men with facial scars more attractive. This might sound weird at first until you connect it with what we previously discussed.

Women seek any cues that show the presence of masculinity, and facial scars are one of these features. Women unconsciously assume that a man with facial scars is braver, stronger, and more masculine.

Even though men don't fight for food these days the way they used to, the way we were designed still makes women find such strong men more attractive.

Another study has shown that women might prefer a man with facial scars for a short-term relationship and one without any for a long-term relationship.

Masculine traits might make a man unable to settle with one woman, while the kind-looking man who has no scars will most likely settle down and take care of their children. That's the reason women prefer men without scars for long-term relationships.

Contrary to common belief, facial scars on women don't affect their overall attractiveness. A woman with a facial scar and a woman without one can be found equally attractive by men.

Facial Hair

You don't need to read the results of any studies in order to figure out that men find women with facial hair less attractive. In general, any sign that shows the presence of female hormones makes a woman more attractive, and vice versa.

That's also why hair on a woman's body is always considered unpleasant except for around the reproductive area, because this shows that a woman is more fertile.

Studies have shown that women tend to prefer men with facial hair, especially a beard. While the recent Western stereotype has been trying to promote a new standard, which is a clean-shaven man, it seems that women still find men with facial hair more attractive.

One study has found that women believe that managers with more facial hair are more competent and in control. A bearded man can appear to be more masculine to women and that's why they might find him more attractive.

This study claims that men can gain an extra edge by growing a beard.

What If You are not their Type

According to the psychology of attraction people don't consider anyone a potential partner unless he meets certain conscious and unconscious requirements.

For example, one of these requirements for a woman might be, "he must be tall," and one of these requirements for a man might be, "she must be blond."

So what if a short man wants to date a woman who is looking for a tall man, or what if a brunette falls in love with a man who is looking for a blond, do they have any chance? Can someone attract another person even if he's not the latter's type?

Yes of course this can happen! But before you know how it can be done you first need to understand how attraction happens.

How attraction happens

A person's subconscious mind can receive the same message through different channels. If a man sees a very beautiful woman, then he might assume that she is popular; if the same man sees an average-looking woman on TV then he will also assume that she is popular.

In both cases the man concludes that the woman is popular, even though he is receiving the message through different channels.

So what does this have to do with attraction?
As I said earlier, people have types because they associate certain traits with certain physical features.

A woman who is looking for a tall man might also be looking for a protective and strong man. Now, once you understand what this woman is looking for, you can show her that you've got it through a different channel.

In such a case, being confident, wealthy, or ambitious will send the same message to that woman through a different channel, and so she might sacrifice the physical height constraint.

A man who is looking for a blond might be an attention seeker who wants to show others that he can win the heart of a popular woman; in such a case if the brunette makes him realize that she is popular as well, then he will forget about his preferred type and go for her.

Understanding why people look for certain types is the key

Your efforts will be in vain unless you know exactly why your target is looking for a certain type. If you understood your target perfectly and knew what traits he has associated with the type he is looking for, then you can show him that you possess these traits even if you are not his type.

Here is a final example. A woman who is looking for a man with masculine looks, because she wants to feel safe, can sacrifice that condition if she knows that another man practices martial arts.

In short, as long as you can send the same message through a different channel, then you can still attract a person even if you are not his type.

The Conclusion

Have You Come Up With a Conclusion Yet?

Do you think you have got attractiveness wrong?

- As you may now realize, the way people perceive attractiveness differs from one person to another, from one culture to another, and even from one day to another.

- While you might be obsessed with the shape of your nose, people may be envying you for your body shape.

- While you might not be in love with your face, people could be in love with your height.

- I know you don't look like a super model but actually no one you know does. Even super models themselves don't look the same in real life.

- If someone tells you that you are unattractive one day, then this doesn't mean that you are not attractive, but it might mean that you look like someone that person resented before.

- A woman might reject you because you approached her on a certain day of her menstrual cycle, while a man might reject you because you remind him of his mother, who he does not like.

- Yes, physical attractiveness is extremely important, but before you start judging yourself make sure you first understand how people around you perceive physical attractiveness.

- The biggest mistake people can make is to look at pictures of models from magazines and assume that everyone will judge you according to them. That's not the case. If these images do anything, it is to lower people's self-esteem even more, and thus give a confident person a cutting edge advantage over others.

- As you may now understand from the studies highlighted in this book, confident people are much more attractive.

- A woman can reject you even if you look good because she is looking for other traits that you don't display, and a man can reject you even if you look good just because of the associations his subconscious mind formed long ago.

- Your personality and everything that is connected with you affect your overall attractiveness.

Be confident by understanding how others really see you and you will become really attractive. If looks represent a part of your overall attractiveness and if you only focus on them, you will end up appearing less to attractive to others.

Instead of focusing on your looks alone, focus on all other factors involved in the attraction process, and your attractiveness levels will shoot up.

PART II
How to Know If Someone Likes You

Extremely Important Notes

The section will help you for sure to know whether someone likes you or not with a hundred percent accuracy, but in order for this to happen you need to take the following few points into consideration:

1) The signs in this section are numerous, and seeing one or two signs is not enough to judge whether someone likes you or not. However, when five or more signs appear, then something is certainly going on.

2) Don't make quick judgments before you learn how to spot all of these signs so that you get correct results. The process of detecting those who like you is fairly simple, but it requires few days of training, so take your time and don't rush things.

3) Some signs have a **much higher weight** than others, and so if only three of them are present then there is a big possibility that the person is in love with you. Throughout the book I will notify you about these signs by using the words **"high weight"** next to some sub-headings.

Are the Signs Listed for Males or for Females?

I usually get mails from people asking me whether the signs I write about are for males or for females. The answer is, the signs are for both sexes unless otherwise stated.

All the signs in this book are for males and for females except for a few special ones that I will point out by mentioning that they work only for a certain sex.

So by whether I am using **she** or a **he** you'll know that I am talking about human beings in general.

Body Language Signs
(The Real Ones)

Why did I Use the Words "Real Ones" in the Slogan?

Simply because when it comes to body language the Internet is full of false information and wild guesses that have no real scientific basis.

All the signs you are going to learn about now are backed up by scientific research and real-life tests.

Because I owned a company that provided training for those who wanted to learn more about personal development topics I managed to carry out live tests on thousands of people who used to attend the courses.

As a result of these tests I managed to filter out the signs that weren't that accurate and to make sure of the ones that made sense the most.

Personal Space (High Weight)

Each person has a circle surrounding him called their personal space. If anyone gets inside our personal space we will feel uneasy, uncomfortable, and tense.

Unless we really feel comfortable being around that person we will quickly step back to bring that person out of our personal space.

Do you know why do people feel uneasy inside elevators? It's because their personal space is overlapping while they barely know each other.

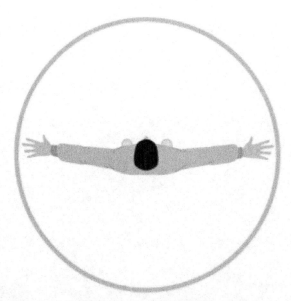

You might have also noticed that close friends always keep smaller distances between each other when standing together than the distances they keep when standing with strangers.

I can easily spot close friends from afar just by looking at the small distance they leave between them. Close friends usually stand and sit very close to each other to the extent that their shoulders or legs might sometimes touch.

When someone likes someone else he will **unconsciously** want to come closer to them, and so he will reduce the private distance between him and that person to the extent that the other person might feel like wanting to step back.

 If you are standing with group of people and a girl likes you then she will be standing as close to you as possible while leaving greater distances between her and the other people.

In short, If someone allows you inside his personal space then the only possibilities are:

1) He likes you.
2) He is interested in you.
3) Or he feels comfortable talking to you or being around you.

 On the other hand, if someone tries to step back whenever you come close to him then this person might not be interested in you, nor does he want to come closer to you.

VIP TIP: Let me remind you of the fact that one sign is never enough for determining whether someone likes you or not. I don't want you to feel bad if you see someone stepping away from you, simply because one sign is never enough to draw a conclusion, even if it is a powerful one.

There is one important thing that I haven't mentioned yet. How can personal space be measured? Of course the size of the personal space varies from one person to another, and that's why you need a method to tell whether a person wants you inside his personal space or not.

In order to test personal space correctly you can step forward while talking to your potential partner and then notice his response. If the person unconsciously pulls back then he might not want you to step inside his personal space.

VIP TIP: When stepping forward you must do this in a way that doesn't allow the person's conscious mind to notice. Most of the signals I will talk about in this book are unconscious signals that happen without the person noticing them.

If for any reason the person notices that he is sending such a signal he might pull back and do the exact opposite!!

For example, if someone notices that he is standing closer to you then he might pull back in order not to show that he is into you.

There is an even better way of doing this test. Instead of stepping forward, just step backward, and see if the other person tries to reduce the distance between you and him once again. If a person likes you he will unconsciously want to stay close to you, and so by pulling back you will be forcing him to take few steps forward.

If you are all seated, the person who likes you might attempt to change his place in order to sit closer to you. Again this is considered a sign that he wants to get closer to you; however, you should never judge him before you notice the rest of his actions that happen after he has sat down closer to you.

If a person leans towards you or if he moves in his chair in order to come closer to you, then you can be sure that he is actually trying to reduce the personal space between you and him.

Contrary to common belief, the whole process of moving closer to someone or pulling back is completely done by the **subconscious mind**, and it has nothing to do with logical thinking or even with noticing what's happening.

Even if a girl is very shy and if she doesn't want to show that she likes you, she will still come closer to you without noticing. If for any reason her conscious mind realizes that she has come too close to you she will pull back for a while then get closer again when her conscious mind forgets about the issue.

I remember one day I was standing next to a girl who liked me, and I noticed she was coming closer and closer. I was 100% sure that she wasn't aware of the fact that she was coming closer because she was a very shy person.

When I took a step back I did it in the wrong way, which made her notice that she was too close. At this point she blushed and pulled back!!

So in short, even a shy person will make this move as long as his conscious mind doesn't notice it.

Orientation

It's almost impossible to talk about personal space without talking about orientation.

What is the difference between the two pictures shown below?

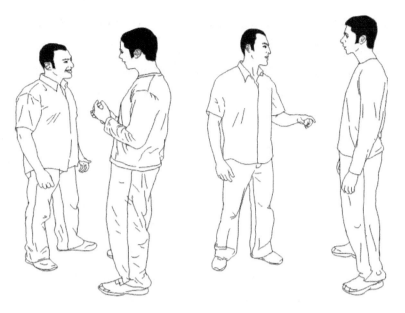

In the first picture (the one on the left), the person is standing with his shoulders parallel to the other person; this is called proper orientation and it happens when the angle between you and the person you are facing becomes zero, while in the second picture the person is standing without facing the other one properly.

As you can see, the guy in the picture on the right is not facing the other guy with his full body, but instead his body is leaning away at a certain angle.

In body language, proper orientation is a signal of interest and of wanting to keep standing with that person. If the person you are talking to is not properly oriented, then this doesn't have any meaning other than he wants to leave.

Of course wanting to leave doesn't always mean that the person dislikes you, but it could mean that he is in hurry or that he has important things to do.

VIP TIP: If a person likes you, but for some reason believes that you don't like him, then he might feel like wanting to avoid you in order to protect his dignity. In such a case this person might appear as if he is in a hurry whenever you talk to him, even though he actually wants to talk to you some more.

Proper orientation is one of the strongest signs of attraction, simply because the person who likes you will want to stand with you more. If you are standing in a group, then it's impossible for every person to orient himself with everyone else, since each person can only face a maximum of two other people, but if someone likes you he will ignore the whole group and unconsciously orient himself towards you.

VIP TIP: Everyone without exception never maintains proper orientation when they are in a hurry. So if you meet someone who doesn't face you with his whole body, then don't jump to conclusions and say that he doesn't like you, simply because he might just be in a hurry!

Even if you are not standing next to a person, or even if he is standing with other people few meters away, he will still face you with his body if he likes you. I can easily notice people who are trying to orient themselves with me, even though they are standing a bit further away from me. First I see the person looking at me to determine my position, then I notice that he is slowly shifting his position in order to end up facing me.

If a person always faces you even though he is standing with other people, then you can be sure that there is something going on.

People's subconscious minds always believe that if they are facing a certain object then they can get to it easily. That's why the subconscious mind of a person who likes you will make him face you. By doing so his subconscious mind will rest assured that it helped him make the first move towards approaching his target.

The reason I didn't write "high weight" next to this sign is that if someone is interested in talking to you due to any other reason, then he will still maintain proper orientation. For example, if you are telling someone about an interesting topic, then maintaining orientation will happen naturally even if he doesn't like you.

VIP TIP: A person might not be oriented towards you because of the angle you approached him from. In order to make sure whether he wants to stand with you or not, just change your position to face him properly and watch for his reaction. If he doesn't move, then most probably he wants to stand with you, but if he changes his position and orientation in such a way that he is no longer parallel to you then be aware that he wants to leave.

Is he Really Interested in Listening to You? (High Weight)

Nowadays lots of people try to fake their interest in a topic by either nodding continuously or by acting as if they are listening while they are not.

In body language there are several unconscious signs that can easily let you know whether someone is really listening or whether he is just faking it.

There is one very important point you should bear in mind; the body language I am talking about throughout this book has its source in the subconscious mind and not in the conscious mind.

This means that a person acting out this body language won't be aware that he is doing so, and in addition it won't have **any relation** to cultural differences.

Thousands of books that claim to be body language books go on to talk about cultural differences and conscious gestures. But here is a question that they never consider: if gestures are made consciously by a person and if he is fully aware of them, then what's the use of trying to predict his feelings through them when he can easily manipulate them??

Yes, I know that even unconscious gestures can be controlled by a very few people who know about them, but most people don't know anything about them, and that's why almost everyone makes them without paying attention.

As you can see in the picture below, this person is extremely interested in what he is listening to because his head is tilted. When we are in a state of receiving information that interests us, our heads become tilted. When we like what we are hearing even more, we might even start to smile while listening.

It's very common that someone makes this gesture when you are talking about an interesting topic, but if someone keeps making it while listening to you even if you are talking about yourself, then you can know for sure that he is interested in you.

I don't want to tell you to depend on this sign alone for the sake of accuracy, but be aware that it's one of the most powerful signs that can indicate whether someone is interested in you or not.

Note that the main sign we are talking about here is the tilting of the head, and that it's usually accompanied by resting the cheeks on the hands as shown in the picture, just to support the body.

The Back Test

Tim was sitting in front of his laptop browsing the Web. While he was online, a close friend of his appeared.

Suddenly Tim's back became straight. A few minutes later his friend left and Tim started to feel a little bored. Without noticing, his back became curved and he slumped back a bit into his chair. After some time, his phone rang and upon answering, he realized that he had to deliver some stuff to his aunt who lived at the other end of town; at this point his back bent even more and he slumped deeper into his chair.

While Tim was thinking about that unexpected errand he had to do, his phone rang again; it was his aunt telling him that she wouldn't be home and so he wouldn't have to deliver the stuff that day. Tim's back became straighter than ever and he felt happy.

When we feel good, confident or interested in something, our backs straighten and we stand tall. On the other hand, when we feel down, less confident, or when we are bored, our backs become curved.

I want you to watch your back for just one day and see when it's straight and when it's curved. You will discover that whenever something good happens your back becomes straighter, and whenever something bad happens your back becomes more curved.

So what does this have to do with knowing whether someone likes you or not??
Simply, if someone likes you then his back will become straight as soon as you arrive or when you are near him as a result of his elevated mood.

If you talk to a person and things don't go well according to his own perception, then most likely his back will become curved right after you leave, and vice versa. If everything goes well when you are with him and he seems satisfied with what's happened, then his back will remain straight even after you leave.

The spinal cord is one of the most powerful indicators of our moods, and therefore you can use this fact to find out whether someone is happy being around you or whether it doesn't mean anything to him.

You can also carry out a test manually by complimenting that person and watching his back and his mood. If he becomes energetic, excited and his back straightens after you leave, then there is a very big possibility that he likes you (of course a friend must be there right after you leave to tell you what happens).

Note that the person may become happy or energetic because of something you said, and not because he is actually in love with you; however by watching for the other signs that were mentioned earlier, you will be able to tell the difference easily.

The straightness of the back is one of the strongest signals that can show that someone likes you; however, you must bear in mind that lots of other factors can contribute to the straightness of the back, and that's why you should take care.

Positive Evaluation (High Weight)

In body language, when you see something that you like, you will usually make a gesture called the "positive evaluation of the situation," which is shown in the pictures below.

As you can see in the picture, when we evaluate something in a positive way we either scratch our eyebrows or return our glasses back to their place (even if they were already in place). In order to get a better understanding of the positive evaluation gesture, let me give you few examples of situations where it might occur:

- When you see a beautiful cell phone that you are about to buy.
- When you read your exam results and find that you got straight A's.
- When you arrive late for a lecture and discover that it was cancelled.

I know what you are thinking of right now; you are wondering what returning your glasses to their place has to do with seeing something that you like?

Simply your subconscious mind believes that returning your glasses to their place will improve your vision, and so allow you to see whatever it is you like more clearly.

When you like something you will feel that you want to scratch your eyebrows as well. Whenever you find yourself scratching your eyebrows, try to recall the last thought that was in your mind and you will discover that it was a positive thought.

Both signs have the same exact meaning; they have no other meaning than liking something. No, you are not returning your glasses back to prevent them from falling off, because if this was case you would never have made this move twice in less than five minutes upon seeing something that you like.

So what does all this has to do with knowing whether someone likes you or not??

Simply these gestures also happen when you see people that you like!!

So if someone makes them :

- Upon seeing you.
- Upon knowing that you will show up in the place he is going to be in the following day.

Then be aware there is a good possibility that he likes you. One important thing you should consider is that the absence of these signs doesn't mean that the person dislikes you, but their presence surely means that he is interested in you.

So in short, if you see these signs then count them as a positive point and if you don't see them then just look for other signs.

This is how body language works. The presence of certain signs is always an indicator of the presence of certain emotions, but the absence of these signs doesn't always reflect the absence of those emotions.

There is a very simple yet extremely effective test that can help you find out whether someone likes your presence or not.

You just need a close friend to mention the fact that you are coming soon in front of your target. If the target makes these gestures, then there is a large possibility that he is happy because you are going to show up.

VIP TIP: Thoughts fly through the mind very fast. If you say several things, then ten different thoughts might quickly pass through the mind of your target, and as a result you might not be able to tell which thought triggered his current body language or gesture.

In order to avoid this problem you need to make sure that the friend you are going to send to make the test speaks slowly and communicates the information bit-by-bit.

Negative Evaluation

Suppose that you come back home feeling very thirsty after a long work day.
What will happen if you open the refrigerator and find nothing at all to drink?

At this point, you're most likely to develop negative feelings towards the situation.

Here is another example that might result in such negative emotions: Suppose that you have an appointment for a job interview and that you are already late.

What will happen if as soon as you arrive at your car you discover that you've left your keys at home?

Most probably you will experience similar negative feelings to the ones you experienced in the first situation.

When a negative situation happens, the blood capillaries in your nose contract, and so you will feel like wanting to scratch it, which in turn results in the gesture shown in the picture below.

This gesture is one of the most common gestures in body language because of the many negative situations we encounter in our lives.

A lot of people, on seeing the picture below, will think that they have never made that gesture before, while in fact they are completely wrong.

The truth is that they've made it thousands of times, but since the gesture wasn't relevant to the subconscious mind, it was always discarded. Now that you are aware of the significance of that gesture you are more likely to notice it the next time you make it.

VIP TIP: The subconscious mind receives millions of pieces of information per second. Because most of this information is not relevant it is discarded, unless it's of interest to you.

You might have been discarding all the information about your gestures just because they meant nothing to you in the past, and that's why you might believe that you've never made a certain gesture before.

So what does this have to do with knowing whether someone likes you or not???
Suppose that someone makes the above gesture right on:

- Finding out that you are interested in someone else.
- Finding out that you won't show up for the next few weeks.
- Being told that someone has proposed to you.

If the person doesn't like any of these situations, then there is a big possibility that he likes you.

There are hundreds of similar statements that you can use intentionally to test whether the target person likes you or not. For example, if you tell your target that you have to leave for one year for another country and that you might not have Internet access there then he will surely make this gesture if he loves you.

Many sources on the Internet incorrectly claim that touching the face is a negative sign, but as you've just seen, touching the eyebrows has one meaning while touching the nose has a completely different one.

In addition, even negative gestures can have a positive meaning if they are made in response to something negative that was said. For example, if someone touches his nose (negative move) upon finding out that you are already committed then this negative move actually has a positive meaning, which is that this person likes you.

Touching the Eyes is also a Negative Sign

People unconsciously touch or rub their eyes when they see something that they don't want to see. The subconscious mind believes that by doing so it will help them avoid seeing it.

The good news is that this gesture also happens when someone visualizes a negative scenario. In other words if you tell a person that you might be travelling for a year, and then he rubs his eyes, then know that he is visualizing a negative scenario in his mind (for example not seeing you for a year).

That's why this is another sign you can use to find out whether someone likes you or not. Note that a person will usually rub one eye or touch it with a finger when he visualizes that negative situation.

Playing With Her Hair, Pulling on His T-shirt (High Weight)

One of the most talked-about signs on the Internet is the hair flip that a woman does when she meets someone interesting. This sign is absolutely true, and it's one of the most powerful signs you can use to find out if someone likes you.

Actually, if a girl likes you a lot she might keep doing this hair flip every now and then as long as she is standing next to you. The presence of this multiple hair flip action alone is a powerful indicator that this girl likes you and at worst she is very interested in you.

This level of interest can easily be then turned into love by applying a few techniques that are based on the psychology of love. In my book, How to make someone fall in love with you, I explained how initial attraction is all that's needed for someone to fall deeply in love with you. All you need to do is to apply a few techniques such as induced excitement, induced addition, subconscious mind programming, and love economics to turn that initial interest into real love.

If there is an initial interest, then making someone fall in love with you is going to be a piece of cake.

So what is the relationship between liking someone and flipping hair? Some psychologists who support the hypothesis that love never happens unless there is some sort of physical attraction believe that this hair toss is an unconscious move done by a woman to reveal some of her hidden skin to the person she is interested in.

Even though I think that there are some cases where love can happen without physical attraction, I still find their reasoning very logical and highly acceptable.

This hair flip is among the most powerful signals that can show whether someone likes you or not. Had I not been afraid that you would form quick judgments I would have told you that this gesture alone is enough to let you know if someone likes you.

The frequency of the gesture is also very important. If the hair flip is done once then you can blame it on the wind, if there was any, but if the girl keeps doing it over and over whenever you are there, then certainly there is something going on.

Another very important gesture that shows whether someone cares about his looks in front of you or not is pulling at his t-shirt right at its bottom just before approaching you.

Guys and girls both do this gesture to stretch their t-shirts so that they look tidy in front of others. Of course this is also an unconscious move that has nothing to do with the conscious desire to look better, but it just happens when someone becomes concerned about his self-image in front of someone else.

If you see a guy doing this right before approaching you then be aware that he wants you to find him attractive and that he cares about his looks in front you.

Another common gesture made by guys when they become obsessed with their looks in front of someone is adjusting their shirt so that they hide their belly fat. Some guys also voluntarily inhale to prevent their belly from showing before approaching someone they are interested in.

In short, if someone's interested in you he will do his best to appear on his best form.

Pointing Hi Toes Towards You (High Weight)

Just as I said before, proper orientation in body language means that a person is interested in you, but there is an additional powerful sign that can help you know whether someone wants to be with you or not even if he is standing with someone else.

I have said that a person who wants to approach you will orient himself in such a way that his body is facing you, but what if that person is sitting down?

What if he can't twist his body for any reason? This is where the next sign comes into play, which is pointing his toes towards you!

It has been found that people point their toes towards the destination they want to go to.

The subconscious mind in this case believes that pointing the toes towards a certain destination will make the process of walking to it easier.

One study has found that people who don't feel satisfied during job interviews point towards the door with their toes. This happens because these people feel like leaving the job interview.

If your target is sitting some distance away then you can easily look at his feet to see whether they are pointed at you or not.

Note that the person won't point at you with both his feet because one of them has to go in another direction so you have to look for only one foot that is pointed towards you.

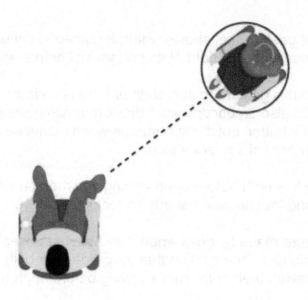

All about Smiles

Almost all websites say that smiling is a sign of interest, and while this fact is correct there are still lots of in-depth details to be considered before you count a smile as a sign of attraction.

Here is why you shouldn't count a smile as a positive sign as soon as you see it:

Does the smile last? Lots of people are nice, they will try to put a smile on their face to pretend that they are happy to see you but it has been found that real smiles last for a few seconds even after the person has looked away. It has also been found that smiles that result from being attracted to someone last even longer.

Examine the smile of a person right after he turns away, or let a close friend do it for you, and you will find out whether this smile is real or fake.

Is it a fake smile? True smiles don't only move the lips, but they extend by moving many of the face muscles. Find a time when you are smiling from your heart, then cover your mouth with your hand and stand in front of the mirror. What you will find is that you still see yourself smiling even though you can't see your mouth.

The clearest difference that can be noticed between a fake smile and a real one is the movement of the muscles surrounding the eyes.

You will notice some wrinkles or movements in the skin around someone's eyes when he is smiling from the heart. If on the other hand the smile is moving the mouth only, then it might be a fake smile. See the picture below:

Vs.

One very important point to note is that a person might be faking a smile because he is feeling bad, or because he's having a bad day and not because he doesn't like you, so make sure you look for all the signs together instead of just the smile.

Smiling for no reason: We usually smile when we hear something interesting or when someone says something funny, but when we become interested in someone we I tend to smile for no reason to the extent that we may keep the smile on our face as long as the conversation is going.

If someone keeps smiling at you for as long as he is talking to you without doing the same thing with other people, then know that there is a very big possibility that he likes you.

All About The Eyes

The Prolonged Gaze

Proper eye contact shows interest. To properly maintain eye contact you need to look to the person you are talking to 70-80% of the time.

Studies have shown that when someone becomes interested in another person he maintains eye contact for a longer period of time.

You might be wondering how a shy person can maintain eye contact for long periods of time?

With shy people this is going to be a bit different. Yes, they might not be able to look you in the eye for long periods of time, but you can easily realize whether they are interested in you or not by comparing the duration of their eye contact when they are with you to the duration of their eye contact when they are with others.

If normal people look at you for two seconds before looking away, then the person who likes you might look at you for four seconds. As soon as he realizes that he is doing it he will shift away his eyes and look somewhere else because of his shyness, but as long as the subconscious mind is taking control then his gaze is going to last for longer periods of time.

Note that looking someone in the eye results in producing the same chemicals that are released when you become attracted to someone.

This is why in my book, How to Make Someone Fall in Love With You, I said that looking someone in the eye for prolonged periods of time can fool him into thinking that he is in love with you.

Pupil Dilation (Very High Weight)

Our pupils become bigger to allow more light in when we are in a dark place. They also become smaller to allow less light in when we find ourselves in places with strong light that can harm our eyes.

These changes don't only happen when light changes, but they also happen on seeing objects that we like or dislike. When we see something that we like, our pupils tend to become bigger in order to allow more light to be reflected from this object and into our eyes.

Research has shown men's pupil's become bigger when they look at nude photos of females. Other research has shown that it's possible to detect gay people by watching how their pupils change when they shift from watching pictures of people of the opposite sex to pictures of people of the same sex.

Yet more research has shown that people's pupils become larger when they are shown pictures of politicians that they like and smaller when they see pictures of politicians they don't like!

So what is the logical explanation for such a change?

Simply because your mind always wants the best for you. When you see something that you like then most probably your mind will make your pupils become larger in order to help you see it more clearly.

When someone likes you, his pupils will become bigger as soon as he sees you, even if the lighting in the room hasn't changed. You must be telling yourself that it's very hard to predict this change, especially since his pupils will always be big while you are there.

Again, you need a friend here who can notice the before and after sizes of the target's pupils and to tell you if there is any difference.

One very important thing to take into consideration is that such a test must be done in the same place, or changes in the light intensity might give false indications.

Bright Eyes

I have also noticed that our eyes shine when we see someone that we like; bright eyes are one of the strongest signs that can show whether someone really likes you or not.

We have small glands in your eyes that secrete fluids that help our eyes function better.

It seems that the subconscious mind likes to improve the function of the eye when it sees someone or something that it likes.

That's why bright eyes can be a sign that shows that someone is interested In you.

Looking at You After Saying Something Funny:

If someone likes you he will do his best to see you smiling or laughing. If he tells a joke that appeals to you or if you like what he said, his mood will change suddenly; he will become happier and more energetic.

If someone likes you he will do his best to make you laugh; that's why he will always look at you right after saying anything funny in order to check whether you are laughing or not.

A person who likes you will give you a look with a smile on his face right after he says the funny thing. It's as if he is telling you, "Hey, I'm trying to make you laugh, did you like it?"

Within a few minutes you can easily determine whether someone is doing this or not because he will simply be repeating it over and over. One important thing you must do is to not laugh out loud every time so that he doesn't become confident enough about his ability to make you laugh and so stop doing the test.

He Will Keep Looking – Eye Contact Distribution:

Generally people distribute eye contact equally among those they are talking to unless someone is found to be more interesting (and so he gets a bigger share of the eye contact).

When someone likes someone else he will want to keep looking at him all the time. This becomes very evident when a group of people are sitting together and the person is looking at one of them most of the time.

Sometimes a charismatic person can take all the limelight, thus forcing your target to keep an eye on him. Just take this point into consideration in case you encounter such a situation.

The other thing to watch for is pupil dilation; do the person's pupils change size when he shifts his sight from other people to you? I know it might take some time before you can train yourself to notice this change, but certainly when you learn it you will get very accurate results.

Looking away when you notice him: If someone likes you then he will try keep his eye on you most of the time. That's why he will change his orientation and face you with his body even if he is not standing with you. Now what do you think will happen if he discovers that you have noticed him?

Most probably he will back off by shifting his sight away immediately in order to hide his intentions and he might even move his body away to face another direction.

If you want to make sure whether someone is trying to keep his eye on you or not, then don't let him notice that you are noticing him. Just leave him alone for prolonged periods and you will easily be able to determine whether he wants to look at you or whether he was looking in your direction by coincidence.

Behavioural changes

Hormonal Changes (High Weight)

Emotions are nothing but chemical reactions and hormonal changes taking place inside the body. Attraction or love is nothing more than the feelings we get when serotonin, dopamine, and phenylethylamine are produced inside our bodies in addition to some other chemicals.

When these chemicals are released inside the body, certain changes can be noticed in the person which reflect their presence. By learning how to spot these changes in someone you will be able to find out if these hormones have been released, and so you will know whether he likes you or not.

Anxiety: The first feeling that someone experiences on the release of these chemicals is anxiety. The anxiety in this case is not similar to the one we experience when we are about to make a presentation because in this case it's mixed with excitement and happiness.

Anxiety is one of the earliest signs that someone experiences when talking to a person he likes, and so it makes the early detection of attraction much easier.

Contrary to common belief, everyone experiences anxiety, even confident ones, because of the powerful effects of the hormones released. However, it happens with varying intensity. You can simply spot a state of anxiety by watching for these signs:

- Making speech mistakes while talking.
- Becoming restless.
- Clumsiness.
- Sweating.
- Raised heart beat and increased rate of breathing (you can easily determine this by looking at the person's shoulder movements; if they start going up and down faster then the rate of breathing has increased).
- Jiggling the contents of the pockets.

Hyperactivity: Anxiety might not last for the whole meeting, especially if the person is confident. As soon as the anxiety fades away happiness remains, which results in a state of hyperactivity. Under the effects of hyperactivity the person becomes:

- Very excited.
- Full of jokes.
- Restless.
- Very happy.
- Very energetic.
- Very motivated.
- Very optimistic.
- More extroverted than he really is.

You can easily notice these changes in state by making note of previous mood changes.

In some cases a person might remain anxious for the whole meeting, and then become hyperactive as soon as the person he likes leaves, provided that the conversation went well.

One of the things that used to let me know if a person likes someone in few minutes was the huge change in mood from dormancy to hyperactivity right after the person he likes has left.

You don't have to do the task yourself of determining whether a person likes you or not, just meet with him with a friend of yours, then leave a few minutes before your friend and let him tell you if he found any signs of hyperactivity right after you left.

Identifying With the Person (Very High Weight)

"Sarah and I didn't like the movie."
"We both hate chocolate cakes, that's funny."
"We are the only people in here who like walking in the rain."

What have all of these phrases got in common?
It's that the person talking is always trying to associate himself with someone else.

The term "identifying with a person" means trying to find something in common between you and then declaring it.

When someone likes someone else without having the chance to tell him, she will usually want to release some of these feelings by any means. One of the most popular ways of releasing excessive feelings of attraction is identifying with the other person.

When someone identifies with someone else and uses the word "We," it gives him a sense of oneness.

This is somehow similar to the feeling he experiences when he declares his love.

As seen in the previous examples, you can identity with a person in his presence (examples 2 and 3), or even if he is not there (example 1).

If a person is too shy to identify with the person he likes in her presence then he will do it right after the person leaves. Again, having a close friend who leaves a few minutes after you can help you realize whether that person is identifying with you in your absence or not.

Mr Nice and Mr Nasty (High Weight)

I get lots of emails from people telling me that they are confused because the people they like treat them nicely one day, then completely ignore them the next, or even treat them badly.

The Mr Nice and Mr Nasty treatment method has only one meaning, which is that the person really likes you. Here is how it goes:

- A person likes you; he then tries to treat you well and show you that you are special.
- After a few days, when this person finds no response from you, he feels that he has revealed a lot about his emotions without getting a positive response from you, so he decides to pull back a little.

- The following day he decides not to even say "hi" just to prove to you that he doesn't care.
- Later on he finds you saying "hi" in a pleasant way, so he becomes encouraged once again to be nice, and so on.

Take it as a rule, we can force ourselves to treat someone badly (for example by ignoring him or saying "hi" in a cold way) but we can't force ourselves to be happy around someone!!

If you find that someone is happy being around you for a day or two, then you find him treating coldly the next day, then be aware that he is faking the cold treatment.

The best thing you can do in such a case is to be nice to him even if you were treated with coldness a day earlier, just to encourage that person to take further steps.

Not all people act this way, but most people do, especially those who are completely unsure of your emotions towards them, which is why reassuring people indirectly can make that behavior disappear.

You don't have to tell a person that you like him in order to hear it back, but you just have to make sure that he is feeling secure, or at least that he is not feeling insecure around you, or he will be nice one day and nasty the next day.

Trick Him into Believing that You Like Him

If someone likes you but is not sure of your emotions towards him, then his thoughts will be swinging between the fear of being rejected and hope.

The more fear controls a person the fewer signs he will reveal and the more he will try to avoid you, while the more hope he feels, the more signs he will reveal and the easier you will be able to find out whether he likes you or not.

So, how can you use this information to find out whether someone likes you or not? Simply all you will have to do, is to give the person extra hope so that you encourage him to show the signs without even telling him that you like him.

For example, suppose you are talking to that person about something. During that time he will have two conflicting thoughts; whether you want to stay with him longer, or whether you want to leave. If you kept starting new topics you will make him feel comfortable and he will start to have hope.

This hope will make him reveal more signs that show that he is interested in you. As I mentioned before in the "Mr Nice and Nasty" section, fear is the main reason for withdrawal and for hiding signs of interest, which is why you should always make the person feel that you are interested in him, or at least that you are not bored.

Whenever the person reveals strong signs, act as if nothing has happened and keep showing that you are interested in him. As long as he remains obsessed by hope instead of fear he will keep revealing lots of signs without sensing any danger.

Giving You What They Never Give to Others

Each one of us has his own way of expressing his emotions and of showing interest simply because we have different personalities, and while there are universal signs that everyone makes to show that he is interested in someone, there are still some other signs that are specific to each person and that can help you find out whether someone likes you or not.

The following are examples of behavioural changes that happen when some people like you:

Narcissists put aside their Egos: Narcissists always follow their Egos whenever they go. Try to tell a narcissist that he is incompetent and you will hear all the words you never wished to listen to. However, when a narcissist likes someone he tends to put aside all of his defences and you will find him treating you nicely.

Type A's will waste their time: Type A's can never waste their time on something that they regard as not being useful. If the person you like is a type A (always in a hurry, always having hundreds of tasks to finish and always doing lots of things at the same time), then be aware that wasting 30 minutes of his time helping you with something means that you are very special to him. Type A's never give others their time unless they really like them. Now what if a Type A stayed up all night working on your presentation for you??

Stubborn people let go of their defences: Stubborn people will let go of their defences and become less stubborn when they like someone. Instead of insisting on their own opinion they will become much more flexible and they will hardly ever be stubborn.

If someone likes you and you know that he is stubborn, try to find out if there is any difference between the way he treats you and the way he treats everyone else.

Spending habits will change: The spending habits of the person who likes you will change instantly; he will take you to nicer and more expensive places and he will insist on paying every time, even if this wasn't the way he used to spend.

Doing Difficult and Time-Consuming Tasks for You

If a person likes you he won't hesitate in doing time-consuming tasks for you, even if he has limited time or even if the task is difficult for him.

Sometimes asking someone directly for help can result in making him agree without wanting to, but if the person likes you he won't even wait until you ask him, but he will offer help as soon as he feels that you need it.

You can also ask a person for a favour and see how he reacts. If he hesitates or tries to find excuses not to do it, then most probably he doesn't like you, but if he happily accepts the task then this means that there is a big possibility that he likes you.

Never Become Bored

If someone likes you he will never become bored and he will never try to leave unless he really has to. On the other hand, if the person doesn't like you he might start becoming bored if you are sitting together for a long period of time.

The person who likes you will always find an excuse to stay longer, while the person who doesn't like you will always find an excuse to leave.

One of the signs that always helps me to find out if a person is attracted to someone else is the desire to stay longer. Some people who usually leave at certain times stay late, then leave after their target leaves.

Some people who should leave because the party is over, for example, try to find any excuse to stay longer.

The one thing that usually makes this sign clearer is that this person leaves shortly after the one he likes leaves.

The same thing can happen online. Some people don't go online often, but as soon as the person they like logs in they change their behaviour. They remain online as long as this person is online.

They also change their schedule so that they come online at the same time as their target.

One of the best tricks I used to have when I had doubts that someone liked me was to appear offline instead of logging off the messenger and watching for that person's behaviour.

Most of the time the person who cares about you will leave right after you leave after waiting for a few minutes to make sure that you won't come back.

Doing His Best to Impress You

If a person who doesn't like you is talking to you he won't care that much about showing you how good he is, and he might even be afraid to show you his positive traits so as not to let you become attracted to him.

On the other hand, if a person likes you he will do his best to impress you and to show you that he is worthy of being loved. He will keep talking about his achievements, his good qualities, and if he is intelligent enough he will tell you that lots of people like him.

Generally, when we like a person we will want to show him our best in order to make sure that we will impress him.

Most people dislike showy people, but the truth is that showy people only show off in front of the ones they care about the most.

People who show off in front of you actually want your approval, and if someone always shows off around you then you can know for sure that he cares about your approval a lot.

Generally We Can Say that the Person will Bypass the Norms

Since I can't list all the examples in the world I can summarize all the points in one item, which is that the person will go beyond his normal behaviour and he will change many of the habits he is used to.

What makes changes in habit very predictable is that it only happens with you and not with anyone else. Noticing how he treats other people of the same sex will surely give you an indication of the different level of treatment you are getting.

As soon as you find someone changing his normal habits when dealing with you then be aware that there is something behind the scenes happening.

Looking For Any Excuse to Talk About You (Very High Weight)

When someone likes someone else he usually tries to talk about her all the time, but since he doesn't want to draw attention to himself, especially in the early stages, he will keep finding excuses to talk about her.

Even if the reason to bring the subject up is to make fun of the person he likes it still might be a very strong indication that he likes him. He just makes fun of that person in order to disguise his real emotions, but the truth is that he wants to talk about her all the time and can't find the right topic.

Just send one of your friends and let him stay with that person for the longest possible period of time and so letting him notice how many times he changes the direction of the conversation to talk about you directly or indirectly. If he keeps asking about you or mentioning your name even by making fun of you then surely there is a great possibility that he likes you.

I was once with a friend who kept making fun of the way a certain girl walked. It was very clear to me that he liked her and it turned out to be true.

There is one point that can help you find out whether someone is making fun of someone else in his absence because he likes him or whether he is doing it just to make fun of him.

Watch out for the person's emotions while talking about the one who is absent. If the person likes the one he is talking about you will find him extremely happy and excited while making fun of him.

That friend of mine was introverted, but whenever he made fun of that girl in her absence he became extremely excited and extroverted as long as he was talking about her.

You are Interesting = You are Attractive

Have you ever spent some time with someone then found that he is really interesting? When we spend time with someone new to us we experience new emotions. If these emotions are positive we say that we like being with that person, and vice versa.

So actually we don't love or hate a person, but we love or hate the emotions that we experience while being with him.

When someone says "I hate driving," it doesn't mean that he hates cars, but it might mean that he hates the stress associated with being surrounded by angry drivers or the boredom of sitting in front of the steering-wheel for hours.

So an interesting person is the one who will make us experience good emotions while we are sitting with him. For every hundred times the "interesting" word is used, ninety-nine of them mean that the person is attractive.

When you sit with someone who is physically attractive, certain hormones will flow around your body making you experience feelings of happiness, even if that person wasn't talking at all.

Have you ever described someone as interesting even though he didn't say anything significant that day?

These hormones that flow around your body give you pleasant feelings that you then associate with that person, and so you end up saying that he is an interesting person.

If someone says that you are interesting then this means that you have a very big chance of making him fall in love with you. Actually, if physical attraction is present then your chance of making that person fall in love with you is almost guaranteed.

You are the Only One Who Knows This

One of the most effective signs for finding out whether someone likes you or not is looking out for the phrase "You are the only one who knows this," or "No one knows this except my mom and you."

When someone tells you a secret and then tells you that you are one of the few people who know it then it only means one thing, that this person is trying to tell you that you are really special to the extent that you are one of the few people who know his deep secrets.

The next time someone tells you "You are the only one who knows this," bear the possibility in mind that he likes you, and if you find a few other signs then be aware that he likes you.

Another very famous phrase that I always hear from people who like me is "I feel very comfortable talking to you," or "I feel comfortable the most when I tell you about my problems."

Yawning!!

There are lots of reasons that could make someone yawn, and while the real reasons for yawning are still unknown, observations have proven that yawning happens when:

- You want to sleep.
- When you are receiving too much information.
- When you are bored.
- When you are not interested in the topic.
- When you think that you can be doing something more interesting than what you are doing now.

Yawning is not a good sign at all; however, it doesn't always mean that the person is not interested in you, but it can mean that he doesn't like the topic you are currently talking about.

Yawning can also mean that the person is not bored, but he has other more important things to do other than listening to you. For example, if someone likes someone else then met you while she was on his way to meet him, then she might yawn if you keep talking for a long period of time.

If the person you like keeps yawning every now and then (and if he does it in more than once a day) then you can know for sure that he doesn't like you.

Rapport is Automatically Established

Have you ever noticed that close friends unconsciously mirror each other's moves? It has been found that people who are familiar with each other and who have known each other for a long period of time automatically mirror each other most of the time.

NLP has a technique which is called "rapport establishment," which can help you create a perceived familiarity with a stranger on an unconscious level just by mirroring his moves.

Rapport establishment can make a person feel that you are familiar to him and thus reduce the fears that might prevent him from approaching you.

It has also been found that rapport happens the other way around; when you become interested in someone you will unconsciously establish a rapport with him without noticing by:

- Mirroring his body language.
- Laughing in the same way he does.
- Using the same words he uses.
- Using the same tone of voice.

If you find that someone is automatically establishing a rapport with you, even if you barely know him, then be aware that he is either feeling very comfortable being around you or that he likes you.

Again, notice that this happens in the unconscious mind, and so the person is never aware that he is mirroring you intentionally.

Preferred Clothes and Preferred Colors Repeat Themselves

When someone likes you he will want to appear in his best shape in front of you. This person will think that he appears to be in best shape when he wears his best clothes, and that's why he will keep wearing them whenever you are around.

Just ask that person about his favourite colors or favorite clothes and notice if he wears them when you are around. The other thing that can reveal whether he is trying to let you like him or not is that he will wear his best clothes if he believes that he might see you by coincidence.

For example, if a friend of yours has told him that you are going tomorrow to the same place, he will most probably wear his best clothes.

Even a false alarm will cause that person do his best to appear in better shape in front of you; actually you can use false alarms intentionally, then send a close friend to notice any changes for you and report them back.

Meeting You by Coincidence: (High Weight)

This is one of the most powerful signs that can indicate whether someone likes you or not. When someone likes you he will do his best to see you, and so he will try to predict the places you go to, then follow you there.

When you start meeting the same person by coincidence a lot, especially after giving him hints about your possible hangouts, then be aware that he might be in love with you.

Another test you can do to further make sure that he likes you is telling him that you will be in a certain place and then seeing whether he appears there or not; even if you didn't go for any reason you can let someone check for you and tell you whether he went there or not.

Sometimes the person might not want to show that he likes you, and so he might not go to the same place, but he will never be able to resist the urge to go to the places you go to if he hasn't seen you for a long time.

Try to be unavailable for few days, then tell him about your movements one day and see whether he appears there or not. Of course you must choose public places so that he has enough courage to show up without the fear of giving away that he came for you.

Conversations Take Longer than Expected

If someone likes you he will do his best to spend as much time as he can with you. He will try to extend a conversation as much as he can by starting new topics whenever a topic finishes.

A very good way to test this is to help him by starting new topics, then waiting for him to talk; if you find that whenever a new topic starts he keeps talking without wanting to leave then be aware that he might be interested in you.

If the person who likes you finds enough topics to talk about he will stay for the longest possible period of time, provided that you don't scare him by showing signs of boredom or lack of interest.

How many times does he use your name?

A person who likes you will most probably call you by your name more often than other people. When someone likes someone else then calling him by name gives him pleasant feelings.

And if for some reason he doesn't to do it, because of being shy for example, then most probably he will keep talking about you for the rest of the day after you leave.

Watch for the number of times a person calls you by your name and compare it to the number of times he calls others by name. Usually a person who likes you will say your name more often.

You will get lots of compliments about your looks

If someone likes you he will usually compliment you a lot, and since love in most cases is based on physical attraction the compliments will most of the time involve the way you look.

It's pretty normal that someone tells you that you look good, but if someone is overdoing it then be aware that he really likes your looks, which is one of the basic essential ingredients for falling in love with someone else.

Compliments will also extend to include lots of other areas, and the person will seem to be more encouraging than anyone else.

His Friends will Know Who You are

If someone likes you he will definitely tell his friends about you, and they will know all the details he knows about you before meeting you.

At the first meeting with them you can very easily determine whether those people already know about you or whether they are just being introduced to you.

If they have been told about you then most probably they will not ask more questions because they already know it all; they won't argue with you because they have already found out about everything you've done, and one of them might even make a mistake that reveals that he/she had received some information about you earlier.

Becoming Interested in Your Hobbies (High Weight)

When someone likes you he will suddenly start to become interested in all of your hobbies. If you tell him that you like drawing he will say that it's a wonderful idea to draw and that you should teach him how to draw one day; if you tell him that you are learning another language he will tell you that he should have done that a long time ago and so on.

In short, if you tell him that you are doing anything he will become interested in it and he will want to join in.

Becoming interested in all of your hobbies and trying to be around you all the time is one of the strongest signs indicating whether someone is interested in you or not.

When is our next meeting?

One of the most important points the person who likes you will bear in mind is the time and date of the next meeting. If you don't mention anything about this then most probably he will come out with something in order to see you once again, such as offering to help you with your studies.

During your conversation with your target you don't have to give strong signs to show that you are interested in him, but you just need to be encouraging and he will do the rest.

The person who likes you will always come up with excuses to meet you again soon, especially if you don't work or study together in the same place.

Finding you nicknames (High Weight)

The person who likes you will usually try to find you a nickname to call you within few days of knowing you.

Because of the intense emotions the person will be feeling towards you that he can't express directly, he will try to find a nickname to call you by to help ease some of these emotions each time he uses it.

So if anybody calls you by a lovely nickname does it mean that he likes you? No, but it means that this person is highly interested in you and again this interest is the main ingredient that is required for love to happen.

Common signs that are correct

Even though most of the websites I mentioned earlier copy the signs from each other without testing their validity, there are still some common signs that they talk about that are correct and that can be used to find out whether someone is interested in you or not.

In order to help you avoid using the incorrect signs I have picked the ones that are correct from the most common ones and have listed them here:

Remembering All the Small Details that You Mention:

If you mention the date of your birthday then the person who likes you will remember it well.

Now if the same topic comes up a few days later you will find that the person remembers the exact date you mentioned.

The same goes for remembering your hobbies, your favorite color, food, the things that you like, and the things that you hate.

If someone likes you he will put very high importance on all the information he can get from you and the result will be remembering all of these small details perfectly.

Never saying no

The person who likes you will hardly ever say no if you ask him for a certain favor, and he will always use such favours as a way of proving to you that he is a good and helpful person.

You will never hear the "I'm busy that day" excuse, or "I'ill be tired after that long work day," but instead all of the difficult and time-consuming tasks will be accepted without question.

One of the best tricks you can use to find out whether someone likes you or not is to send a friend of yours to ask for a time-consuming favour on a busy day, and when the person refuses you can go and ask for a similar favour a few hours later; if the person agrees then there is a big possibility that he likes you.

VIP TIP: Beware of people who know how to attract others. Some people are already aware that confusing a person is the best way to make him think about them more often. People who know such facts might become distant intentionally and might do the opposite of what I just said just to confuse you even more.

Cancellations (High Weight)

If someone likes he will give highest priority to the hangouts where he can see you, especially in the early stages when there is little chance of seeing you. This person will always cancel his plans and delay his appointments in order to be with you.

Even though this sign seems pretty logical, it's one of the strongest indications that someone is doing his best to be with you.

Calling for silly reasons (very high weight)

Try to be absent for few days or to not come into contact with the person who likes you, and he will find any excuse to call you, even if it is a silly one.

One of the ways that can help you make sure if that person is calling for that reason, or if he was calling just to check on you is to not reply with closed-end answers, but rather to encourage him to talk; if the phone call takes longer than expected and if he keeps starting other subjects then know for sure that he isn't calling you because of that silly reason.

The person who likes you will also try to find any excuse to see you if you have been absent for a few days. Suddenly he will become interested in what you do, by studying with you or by helping you with your work.

Raising the Eyebrows

When someone likes someone else he might raise his eyebrows the moment he sees her for the first time. The person will only make this gesture if he is impressed by what he sees.

This is a micro-gesture, and it only lasts for a second, or even less, but a well-trained eye can easily notice it. Try it on yourself first and when you become used to it, start noticing it on others.

Of course if more than one sign appears at the same time, then that would be a strong indication that the person likes you; for example, if the eyebrows were raised, if he made the positive evaluation gesture, and if he stood close to you then the possibility that he likes you will be much higher.

He will notice slight changes to your appearance

If someone likes you he will become obsessed by your physical appearance in such a way that he will notice any slight changes that happen to you (like a new haircut for example).

People who see you every once in a while can easily notice any differences in your looks, but those who see you on regular basis can easily miss the small changes. If someone likes you he will be paying extra attention to these details, and he will notice the slightest changes easily.

Asking More Questions (High Weight)

While this seems like a simple sign, it's still one of the most accurate signs out there that can help you find out whether someone is interested in you or not.

If someone is interested in you then he will certainly keep asking you questions to find more out about you.

Questions such as, "What do you do for a living" when accompanied by the body language statement of interest (tilted head) while listening to the answer can be a very powerful combo that shows deep interest.

Of course any person can ask you questions like that, but only those who are interested in the answer are the ones who care about you. Some people ask these questions as a part of a casual conversation that takes place when you meet them; those aren't the people you are looking for.

VIP TIP: Just as the number of signs you notice is a powerful signal, the intensity of the signs is a powerful signal as well. Sometimes I know that a girl likes me because of the number of questions she keeps asking me on a first meeting.

Minding your own business

"You know what, you would look way better if your hair was curly."
"This shirt will definitely look great on you."
"Why don't you try wearing brighter colours, they will make you look better?"

It's clear that these suggestions are coming from someone who wants to see you in better shape. When someone likes someone else he will start to mind that person's business as well as his own.

Usually this begins in the form of advice about the way you look then it could extend to include other areas like work and study.

Normal friends can make such recommendations, but people who like you won't only recommend such changes, they will do their best to help you follow them.

For example it's not uncommon for a girl who likes you to tell you that tomorrow you should go out together to pick out some new clothes for you.

Interested in everything you do

If someone likes you he will become interested in everything that you do. As I said before, the state of interest in body language can be determined by a titled head, excitement, proper orientation, and proper eye contact.

If the person appears to be interested in all your activities then he might be interested in you. If a person doesn't like you then he will show interest in certain activities and show a lack of interest in other ones that don't interest him.

Again, the state of interest will happen on an unconscious level, which means that the person won't be faking interest in your hobbies, but he will actually become interested in everything that you do.

Final Words

As you have seen, physical attractiveness is not about the face, the shape of the nose, or having a perfect body, but it's all about a combination of many elements that are processed in a certain way according to the receiver's perception.

This is why believing that you are ugly or unattractive is a totally incorrect belief. Surely there are people out there who might not like your looks, but as you have seen, this can happen because of their past experiences, or even other psychological factors that aren't related to you.

Surely there are some people out there who think that you are attractive, so be confident and believe in yourself.

CPSIA information can be obtained
at www.ICGtesting.com
Printed in the USA
LVOW03s1111060416

482422LV00013B/122/P

9 781500 759810